LITTLE VICTIMS

LITTLE VICTIMS

Maurice Richardson

ANDRE DEUTSCH

FIRST PUBLISHED 1968 BY
ANDRE DEUTSCH LIMITED
105 GREAT RUSSELL STREET
LONDON WC1
COPYRIGHT © 1968 BY MAURICE RICHARDSON
ALL RIGHTS RESERVED
PRINTED IN GREAT BRITAIN BY
EBENEZER BAYLIS AND SON LTD
THE TRINITY PRESS
WORCESTER AND LONDON

SBN 233 96052 X

LITTLE VICTIMS

I

'The verse for tomorrow,' said Bobby Gooch, 'is "What shall it profit a man that he gain the whole world and lose his soul." We've got to know it by breakfast.'

Bobby, in his fawn dressing-gown, looked like a plump field mouse. He was homesick but not as homesick as I was for it was not his first term. I had been in tears more or less continuously since arriving at the school. Bobby came from Essex where my family had lived for the first seven years of my life. I imagined he had been asked to keep a look-out for me. We were in the same dormitory, 'New Zealand'; all the dormitories were named after British colonies. I brushed my teeth at my pitch-pine wash-stand and looked out of the window at Brighton and Hove and the sea. It was still quite light, the time being seven-thirty on a May evening, the first of my first summer term in nineteen-sixteen. I was eight years and eight months old. I knelt down and said my prayers which consisted of that rather mawkish oration:

> *Jesus, tender shepherd hear me*
> *Bless thy little lamb tonight;*
> *In the darkness be thou near me*
> *Keep me safe till morning's light . . .*

and one that ended with 'God Bless Mummy and Daddy and Pat (my sister) and Mary (my half sister) and Sandy (my bull-dog)'. The tears were now streaming down my face. They plopped into the po as, still kneeling, I did my final pee. I got into bed and fell asleep surprisingly quickly. Before I left Mowden I broke several school records but the one I broke first was the record for homesickness. Next morning at breakfast I was crying into my cocoa and for the first three weeks of that term, the summer of 1916, I cried at intervals until my parents came down to take me out.

My father, Maurice Henry Richardson, was one of a large Victorian family who had moved to London from Yorkshire – I believe they originally came from Durham – in the eighteenth century. They are described in the County history of Yorkshire as 'this interesting but eccentric family'. My father had five brothers and four sisters. His closest friend among his brothers was Woodhouse who got a KCB for organising Kitchener's supply columns during the Boer War and has been described as 'the greatest quartermaster since Moses'. His eldest brother, Guilford, was a brilliant mathematician and a scholar of Trinity College, Cambridge. He was expected to be senior Wrangler but a week before his tripos he got drunk, visited a red-light district which then – in the late 1870s – existed near the railway station. As he went up to Cambridge when he was only seventeen, it was possibly the first time he had ever got drunk and I should think almost certainly the first time he ever had a woman. I expect it was the last too, because the poor fellow caught a frightful dose of syphilis which came out just before his tripos. He was eleventh Wrangler, not bad under the circumstances, but he never recovered and died when he was about thirty-five.

My father's father, Guilford Barker Richardson, was more than eccentric and I and my cousin, John Richardson, son of Woodhouse, always refer to him as 'the mad dwarf'. He inherited a splendid family business, Richardson and Co, Publishers, Booksellers, Printers, Stationers, Bankers, and East-India Agents. He neglected this business and insisted on devoting himself in an honorary and entirely unpaid capacity to the affairs of the London Metroplitan Water Board. At one time Captain Maryatt, the author of *Mr Midshipman Easy* and *Peter*

Simple, devised a new code of naval signals. My grandfather was about to publish it when the Admiralty intervened. They wrote to him and told him they were taking over Captain Maryatt's code of signals for the Navy and that therefore he could not publish it, but they proposed to compensate him by giving him Admiralty publishing and printing work to do. Instead of accepting this offer, which could have meant a fortune for himself and his descendants, he wrote back and said: 'This is an interference with the liberty of the subject. I'll see you damned. I intend to publish.' The Admiralty restrained him with an injunction and presumably decided that a man so blind to reality couldn't be trusted to publish a laundry list.

Another of his eccentricities took the form of striking his sons at dinner, even when they were all grown up, if they said anything of which he disapproved. He would sit at the head of his table at 61 Shooters Hill Road, Blackheath, with a light Malacca cane beside him with which he would lash out whenever he felt like it. One day his sons took counsel together and said: 'Father, your habit of still striking us now that we are all more or less grown up is undignified. You really must stop it.' He growled: 'I'll see you damned.' The next night at dinner, when he lashed out at his son Oswald who had disagreed with him about his weather forecast, the sons stood up and carefully and as gently as possible took hold of him and held him up in the air. They said they would not put him down until he promised never to strike one of them again. He growled: 'Put me down, damn you,' and rushed for his stick; they took it away from him and up he went again. This time he said: 'Very well I promise.' They put him down and he slunk from the room and wasn't seen again that evening. Next morning he was quite happy chasing across the heath boys whom he suspected of stealing his apples. He died long before I was born but from my father's accounts of him I am inclined to class him as a case of either chronic hypomania or, at any rate, a markedly hypomanic temperament. His wife was gentle and long-suffering;

she wrote a little children's book called *Tales of my Grand-mother's Monkeys*. A liking for monkeys and a feeling of close affinity with them seems to run in the family.

My father was born in 1857. Owing to his father's neglect of his business he had to leave school at Blackheath when he was sixteen and ride a pony from Blackheath to the Stock Exchange to lick stamps in his uncle's office. He was a very strong man physically and though only five feet ten and a half inches tall he weighed twelve stone when he was sixteen. He played rugger for Blackheath as a forward and was tried for England. He married his first wife, Florence Swift, when he was only twenty. She was the barmaid at Cannon Street Station. They had two sons and two daughters, all now dead. One of the sons, my half-brother 'Archie', had a very fine record in World War One and got the MC on the Somme and a bar to it in Mesopotamia. My father broke away from his uncle (who had a typically eccentric son, Murray, who suffered for a time from the delusion that he was engaged to one of Queen Victoria's daughters and that the Prince of Wales was having him watched)* and set up on business on his own as a jobber. He very nearly went smash at thirty; with four children, he was £1,500 in debt. His brother Woodhouse lent him his savings and he turned the corner and began to make money. In 1895, the great boom year, he made over £50,000 dealing in De Beers. I think he got good advice from his great friend Ernest Mocatta. He often used to say to me: 'Always do business with good Jews. A good Jew's idea of a bargain is a transaction which benefits both sides. Some gentiles try to be too smart. As for Greeks, well, you know what they say on the Stock Exchange: "Count your fingers when you shake hands with a Greek".'

My mother was Anglo-Irish. She was the daughter of

---

* Murray Richardson got a first in history at Oxford. His delusion came on quite late in life and he eventually recovered from it. My mother told me he gave her a vivid account of his interview with the Old Queen: 'And being a man of irreproach-able character and not bad-looking, as you know, she approves the match'. He was in fact exceptionally ugly.

William Lane, who was manager of the Munster County Bank in Clonmel, County Tipperary. His paternal ancestors had inherited land from a Cromwellian but I think they had gambled it away and their house, Lane's Park, was burned down; the fire was supposed to have been started in the owner's bedroom; he fell asleep reading in bed and had left his candle alight too near the bed curtains. The Lanes came originally from Shropshire.

During the Civil War there were two brothers. One, a Colonel Lane, fought for the King, and his daughter, Jane Lane, helped Charles II to escape after the battle of Worcester. The other brother fought for Parliament and was given land at Fethard, near Clonmel, by Cromwell.

My mother's father William Lane was by all accounts a very genial pleasure-loving man and my aunt told me that she thought he spent more time in the club and out hunting than in the bank. Some time in the late eighties a swindler descended on the town of Clonmel and took a lot of people for a ride. One of them was my grandfather. He had to resign from the bank and died soon afterwards. He left his widow and her two surviving daughters, my mother Lucy, and her sister Geraldine, always known as Puck, with about £250 a year for the three of them. They moved to Blackheath. My grandmother, whose name was Power, went into widow's weeds and became a prematurely old lady although she lived to be eighty-eight. The dutiful Puck lived with her to look after her. My mother trained as a nurse. Later, she nursed my father's first wife who was dying of consumption, and afterwards married him. She told me after my father's death that she had never been in love with him but had always been fond of him because he was so kind and dependable. He, I think, was very much in love with her.

My father had three sisters living in Blackheath and I suspect that two of them, anyway, tried to high-hat my mother, the former Nurse Lucy who had made such a good catch, my father being then at the peak of his prosperity. My mother, incidentally, was ten years younger than my father. My mother, egged on by my aunt, hit back by saying that all the Richardsons except my father were pompous and selfish. I remember my aunt saying to my mother, when I was very small: 'Be careful now, Lucy, or he'll turn into a regular Richardson.' Another time we were staying in a rented furnished house in Budleigh Salterton which belonged to a sister of Colonel Durnford who got slaughtered by the Zulus at Isandlwana. There was a family crest hanging on the wall with the motto *Sibi Solum.* 'That,' said my aunt, 'ought to be the motto of the Richardsons.' My father took all this sniping in his stride, but in me it produced a curious sense of dichotomy or schism. I did not realize the full significance of it until half a century later during the course of three years' psycho-analysis with Dr Charles Rycroft. Throughout the first fourteen years of my life, including my prep-school period, I almost literally adored, or thought I adored, both my parents.

In 1903 my mother gave birth to a daughter, Pat, who died tragically when she was twenty-three. My father and mother were then living in a large house in Blackheath. In 1904 he moved to Essex, to a house called Redgates in the village of Springfield, just outside Chelmsford. Here I was born on August 24th, 1907. Architecturally it was hideous, but it was very comfortable inside, with large rooms and an Edwardian conservatory opening onto the garden. There were sixteen bedrooms and my parents had eight indoor servants including an angelic Irish cook, Lena O'Donohue, from Middleton near Cork. She was a wonderful cook and I think she was paid about £30 a year. The garden ran to around eight acres including a large vegetable garden. My father was himself a passionate gardener and spent as much time as he could spare growing flowers and rare shrubs. He had a head-gardener named Martin, a dour old fellow with a bushy beard, and an under-gardener, Prentice, who was a Christian Scientist. My father who was by way of being a rationalist agnostic would argue fiercely with

Prentice. He had two motor-cars and he and my mother hunted with the East Sussex. So I suppose I would have to describe myself as a rich man's son.

In 1914 my father sold Redgates to the first Bishop of Chelmsford, Dr Watts-Ditchfield. There was a billiard room in a ridiculous tower.

'I don't need a billiard room but I could turn this into a dormitory to house my ordination candidates,' said the Bishop when my father was taking him over the house. 'What is along that corridor?'

My father told him that along that corridor were the bed-rooms of the maidservants.

'Too near,' said the Bishop. 'Women's bedrooms, too near.'

My father said: 'I must say, Bishop, you don't seem to have much faith in the chastity of your ordination candidates.'

The sale went through. Years later, I said to my mother: 'Mummy, I suppose Daddy must have lost a lot of money when the 1914 War broke out?'

She said: 'No, he didn't. Actually, he hadn't been doing too well on the Stock Exchange for the last few years and needed to economize. But what you don't realize is the difference between prices before 1914 and after. During all the time we lived at Redgates your father's income – and I know because I kept all the housekeeping accounts – was never more than £4,000 a year at the most.'

I tell you this to show you the difference between upper-middle-class standards of living then and today.

In most ways my childhood seemed idyllic. My father, mis-takenly because you should never confuse a child about his identity, had me christened Maurice, his own name, but I was never called by it. Our Irish chauffeur, King, soon after I was born asked my mother: 'And how is me Lad coming along?' and for as long as my parents lived, I was invariably called by them either Lad or even The Lad. I suffered from this nick-name, and even today it embarrasses me. The only other Lads

I ever encountered were invariably failures; one was a champion alcoholic.

I had a nanny, Ethel Skinner, to whom I was devoted. I can remember her wheeling my pram in all weathers wearing a brown bonnet with brown velvet strings tied under her cheeks. 'Never mind the weather Love, so long as we're together Love', she used to hum to me. Her father was a Suffolk game-keeper and he stuffed and mounted a stoat which she gave to me; it stood on the piano in the day nursery and I deluded myself that it was alive. Nanny Skinner undoubtedly spoiled me. She fed me on enormous quantities of very plain food. My half-sister Mary told me afterwards that she had never seen a child eat as much meat as I did. For sweets I was only allowed Velma Suchard chocolate and sometimes 'Hundreds and Thousands'. My favourite tea was sponge cakes with black currant jam on them. Nanny Skinner I now realize, was a bit of a puritan. I think she tried to mould me in her own image. I used to have terrible nightmares of witches from which I would wake screaming. Once, when Nanny was away on holiday, I had the worst nightmare of all. First, I dreamt that witches had spat at me through the bars of a lift. This was precipitated by a visit to London. Next morning in the nursery the following dialogue took place:

Pat: You had another of your dotty fits last night, and Daddy had to leave the bridge party and read you *Jemima Puddleduck*.

Myself: Yes, I know. I had a bad dream. I dreamed that witches spat at me.

Pat: Those are the Essex-spitter witches. You'd better be very careful.

I have often wondered since whether my sister had conceivably collected any of the local witch-lore. Essex was famous witch country and in the early seventeenth century there was a classic witch trial at Chelmsford and another at Castle Hedingham.

The other nightmare was more significant. I dreamed that I

went into a hut, which was just like the summer-house in the garden. Nanny was with me. There were three old women sitting around a table drinking cups of tea. I became very frightened and said: 'Nanny, Nanny, these are witches! Take me away.'

'Oh no they are not,' said Nanny. 'They're just dear old women.'

They gave her a cup of tea and she nodded over it and fell asleep. I woke screaming with terror.

During a bout of psycho-analysis I discovered, though these things are impossible to prove, what I think is the correct interpretation of this dream. I mentioned it to the analyst and he asked me what it suggested to me.

I said: 'Well, in the first place, I always think that the situation in which a person is betrayed into the powers of evil by the negligence of somebody in whom they trust to protect them is one of the most frightening situations imaginable.' I went on to remember the ridiculous, perhaps, but very alarming scene in *Dracula* when Miss Lucy Westenra's idiotic mother comes into her bedroom and tears down the garlic wreathes which Dr van Helsing has put up to keep out the vampire, because they have such a horrible smell.

The analyst agreed that this type of situation was undoubtedly terrifying but he pointed out, with an analyst's tact, that I was only associating to the manifest content of the dream. In dreams, the principal figures are generally persons the dreamer knows in real life but who appear in disguises. . . .

I said: 'Well, I think I can identify the three "witches". They stand for three of my mother's servants. The cups of tea were exactly the same as the cups from which our servants would be drinking tea in the kitchen at their elevenses. But I suppose the chief figure in the dream, apart from myself, was Nanny and she appeared in her own guise. So where does that get us? Unless' – and then I had an inspiration – 'Nanny was the chief witch all along. Yes, by God, I believe that's it.' This was the most dramatic single moment in analysis.

We had been discussing Nanny Skinner and her influence on me for several sessions. A recollection I had had about a childrens' book in which there was a Humpty Dumpty figure, very cosy, a talking egg, with whom I had identified, put us on to the role of Nanny as a retarding influence. I fancied myself as her little egg and she protected my snug fragility from the world. I had remembered, as I mention further on, that the only time I ever saw Nanny angry was when I ran on ahead with a little girl on a morning walk. But this dream, now interpreted, revealed Nanny – that gentle, conscientious, devoted person – as a witch, a dreaded castrator. If so, it's not so surprising that when she did leave I missed her far less than my parents had expected, though they put this down to my love for Sandy, the bulldog, which they had given me as a compensation.

What an odd figure she was, the Edwardian Nanny, who took all the brunt of infancy while darling Mummy ran the house and amused herself. There was something sexless about her, a eunuchoid quality that you would expect to find in a female Origen. The effect on a child of the closest possible contact during those years with a devout puritan – for my Nanny was certainly that – must have been enormous. She was such a kind creature that even now I feel a faint twinge of guilt at writing about her like this. It's difficult to rebel against a paragon of charity and loving-kindness who feeds one like the Good Shepherd and indulges one's megalomania on condition that one surrenders. I think some children feel a need for guiltless hate. David Copperfield was in some ways lucky to have such a monster for a stepfather as Mr Murdstone into whose hand he could sink his teeth with justification.

My relations with my sister Pat weren't too good. We were quite fond of each other in spasms, but my mother was inclined to spoil me at her expense and she was always a rather tempestuous child. I, in my turn, was a bit jealous of her, partly I think because I thought my father preferred her to me.

I was brought up religiously in Church of England style, but religion always depressed me to the depths. I had a book of bible stories illustrated by engravings, among them Elijah – or was it Elisha? – in the Valley of Dry Bones. A thunderstorm seemed to be piling up. This landscape I had always associated with melancholia. Round the age of five, attempts were made to take me to church at Springfield. I used to burst into tears so it was arranged that instead of going to church I should go for a Sunday morning walk with my father. I was never frightened of the devil, I thought of him as a friendly, mischievous imp who might pop out of the oven at any moment.

I was a precocious, rather reserved child. I liked to try to identify myself with grown-ups. One day, when Nanny was wheeling me in my pram, my sister and her governess, Miss Fenner, came by on their ponies. Miss Fenner asked Nanny if she thought it was going to rain? From my pram I piped up: 'In all pwobability it will, Miss Fenner.'

I first fell in love at the age of six, or less, with a little girl named Evelyn Wood, a contemporary of my sister's, whom I secretly adored the moment I saw her at a dancing class in Chelmsford. Another contemporary of my sister's of whom I was fond was Betty Blake, the daughter of the Governor of Chelmsford prison. Her father, Major Blake, was one of the old school of retired army officer prison governors, relatively humane, I should think, but not over-industrious. He was a member of the Garrick Club and spent many of his afternoons playing bridge there. The only way his deputy governor could get him to attend to his prison duties was to telephone an urgent message that a prisoner had escaped. Major Blake would throw down his hand with a curse and catch the next train from Liverpool Street. His deputy would tell him: 'It's all right, Major, we've recaptured him. But now you are here would you mind signing these forms?'

Betty was a dear little girl, lively and friendly. I don't think I ever associated her consciously with the gloom of prison, though in one of my novels I invented a scene in which she told me they were hanging a man that day. We used to play together in a hay field and when I wanted to pee she took a delight in helping me button and unbutton my trousers; she called my penis 'pumpy'. Almost the only time I ever remember Nanny Skinner being cross with me was when, on a winter morning walk, Betty and I ran on ahead crashing our feet through the cat's ice on the puddles in the lane.

In August 1914 my passion for reptiles and amphibia was at its height. My favourite reading was the volume on Reptiles in the Rev. J. G. Wood's *Natural History*. I never caught a lizard or a snake in Essex, but I did have one traumatic experience. My father brought me down from the Army and Navy Stores, of which my uncle Woodhouse was now the Managing Director, a magnificent Dalmatian lizard. We set it loose in the greenhouse and it darted about catching flies. On the second day of its stay old Martin, the gardener, accidentally trod on its tail, high up, and it died. I was inconsolable for three days. I made do with collecting crested newts and those sinister looking black newts with orange spotted bellies; I caught them in our garden pond and kept them in a large zinc tub. I caught them in a net. The crested newts I would spot as they came swimming and pouting up through the bottle-green water with their beautiful crests undulating as they swam. I had no fear of them and picked them out of the net by hand, taking care not to squeeze their slippery little forms too tight. I was more cautious with the big jet black newts; I had a feeling they just possibly might be in some way venomous; but I much admired their marvellously strongly coloured orange and black speckled underbellies. They combined beauty and ugliness in a pristine way.

Soon after the war broke out. The officers of a battalion of sappers were billeted on us and on my seventh birthday they gave me a multi-bladed pocket-knife and a clockwork steamer. The one I was most attached to was the doctor, a grave Irishman named Carr. My sister, who was already mad about horses and had been 'blooded' and given the brush, much to my envy, chummed up with the vet. When we moved out of Redgates my father took a furnished house – Orchard House – in Blackheath. I went to a day school, Belmont, in Blackheath and liked it. I fell half in love with two mistresses. One was Miss Openshaw, the Headmaster's sister, who looked, so I now think, faintly Russian and wore pince-nez; she used to read us *Kidnapped* after tea. The other was Miss Page, an attractive, rather strong-looking young woman, who taught maths. In the spring of 1915 we went to Budleigh Salterton for the Easter holidays and took a furnished house near the golf course. Here, in a patch of heather at the edge of a wood, long since built over, I saw my first adder and caught my first lizard. I took him back to London in a cigarette tin and he was released in the garden of Orchard House.

That winter my parents moved to a glorified boarding house, Colonnade House in the Paragon, overlooking the pond where model-yachtsmen sailed their boats. While the move went on I stayed for a week-end as a boarder at Belmont and cried a little. Mowden was getting very near now. The Snell family who ran the school, had started it in Essex and some of my parent's friends had sent their sons there. One of these sons was Tom Falkner, son of Newstead and Irene Falkner. She was my mother's closest Essex friend, a tremendously sporting lady of the old school who clipped her g's and went on riding to hounds until she was past seventy. And so, in May 1916, I was handed over by my father at Victoria Station to A. P. Snell, the brother of B. A. Snell, the Headmaster, and got into one of the compartments reserved for Mowdenians.

2

The school was just off Dyke Road in a turning then called
Tongdean Lane half-way down which was Tongdean Farm,
now vanished, from which you could walk up onto the downs.
The school building was white rough cast with a brick-tiled
roof; there was a bottom and top storey bow-window and a
gravel terrace. As I never tire of reminding Peter Quennell, the
architect was his father. The classrooms were light and airy,
some of them with parquet floors; the walls were lined up to
half-way with glazed tiles. A long corridor ran the entire length
of the building past the classrooms, the diningroom, and the
studies of A. P. and B. A. Snell. Mrs Snell had her own
drawingroom at the back of the house close to the private
staircase.

From the hygienic point of view it was much superior to my
public school, Oundle, when I went there in 1922. We had a
changingroom with basins and two showers. Upstairs was a
double bathroom where we had cold baths every morning.
We always had a hot bath once a week and a showerbath after
football in winter. I don't suppose, at that period, any small
boys could have been much better looked after so far as their
physical health was concerned. There were in effect, two
matrons for some forty-five boys. One was Mrs Snell, B.A's
wife, about whom I'll have much more to say. The other was
Janet Snell, spinster sister of B.A. and A.P.

Janet was a character, yet not, I think, a genuinely characterful one. She was a tall, rather gawky woman with a russet-
apple face. In 1916, when I arrived, she was wearing the clothes
and hats of ten years before and she was still wearing them when
I left. She was kind within her limits, and conscientious. If a

boy was ill she would spot it at once and if necessary take him to Mrs Snell for consultation. At meals she presided over the new boys' table. I found her conversation very limited. Cricket was her passion and once at the Essex County Cricket ground she had performed a remarkable feat. The batsman hit a six which travelled at high speed a few feet above the ground straight for the nearest spectators among whom Janet was sitting. She stretched out her long rangy arm, caught it in her horny paw and held it. Her only parlour trick that I remember was her sense of smell. She once showed us how she could pick out her own pillow from a pile of others. This feat was quite unaided by any artificial substance, for Janet, I am certain, never dreamed of using scent or any cosmetic. The idea of her dressed up in any way, Janet in drag, is a fantasy.

Mrs Snell was a short, not uncomely lady with a cottage-loaf figure but quite a neat waist. She was brisk and cheerful. I think she was, like her husband and brother-in-law, the child of a clergyman. She played the harmonium at prayers and gave us singing lessons. Some of us never really took to her for in spite of all her geniality she gave us a feeling of slight insecurity; we felt she was an intriguer, and that she and A. P. Snell, with whom she always sat at lunch, used to sway the retiring B. A. Snell, setting the disciplinary trend of the moment, ruling indirectly like a weak King's powerful consort. She not only superintended all the running of the school but also kept the accounts. Without her, I now think, chaos might have supervened.

B. A. Snell, the Headmaster, was oddly old fashioned. Summer and winter he wore a gladstonian collar. He had a distinguished face and a lock of grey hair that sometimes came a little way down his forehead. He was a classical scholar – Jesus, Cambridge – and taught the sixth form and occasionally the juniors. He was inclined to thunder at boys when they were stupid or negligent but he was not an unkind man though on one occasion, as the result of his puritan streak which was very

marked, he behaved, to my mind, abominably. I learnt early
on that he abhorred any even remotely anatomical reference.
On the wall near the library were two pictures by Studdie or
some such comic artist of the period, both of an urchin type of
boy batting at the wicket. One was captioned 'The Hope of his
Side', the other 'Out First Ball'. Passing these one day in my
first term I said: 'The soap of his hide'. A boy who was with me
who had been at the school one or two terms hissed: 'Don't let
BAS hear you.' (He was always known as BAS, pronounced
'Baize'.) This staggered me even then.

I doubt whether BAS much enjoyed being a schoolmaster.
He liked whenever possible to retire to his study and was very
fond of carpentry. Later, he took to keeping Alsatians. When
I revisited the school during my cousin John's time there, I
made some feeble joke about Alsatians recapturing runaway
boys and BAS was not in the least amused. His only contribu-
tion to games was running the shooting on the miniature rifle
range with BSA 22's and, for very juniors, air-fliers. His most
dashing effort in all the time I was there was to buy a Douglas
motor-bicycle and sidecar. I can see him now, wearing a green
cloth cap and his perpetual gladstonian collar, setting off from
behind the carpenter's shop with Ma Snell in the sidecar.

A. P. Snell, known of course as the Ape, was the games
master and taught the fifth form. He had been, like his brother,
to Haileybury and Cambridge, and I think he was a double
blue, rugger and cricket. He was a good deal more sophisticated
and worldly than B.A. He was a good-looking man with a
strong aquiline nose and a rather thin mouth, who dressed in
old greenish tweed suits. His shoes were untidy, yet there was
a faint, very faint touch of – not real distinction but, possibly,
to use that strange word which comes from the same root as
'grammar', glamour about him. Whereas BAS tried on the
whole to be scrupulously fair, the Ape had favourites, liking
pretty, rather dashing little boys. He was married, quite hap-
pily I imagine, to a not unattractive rather governessy-looking

little person called Amy, yet he plainly had a crypto-homo-
sexual streak. This I think he kept very well under control, so
much so that he might almost have had insight into it, though
I can't believe he did.

Apart from his favouritism, the only overt evidence, if you
can call it evidence, of the Ape's homosexuality is a story told
me years later by Tom Falkner, the other Mowden boy from
Essex and a childhood friend of mine. 'One morning in winter,'
said Tom, 'it was devilish cold and we were sitting with our
hands inside our shorts and vests to keep them warm. You
remember those winters and the bloody great blue chilblains.
Well, when the lesson was over the Ape had us all up in front
of his desk one by one and put a hand down each of our trousers and felt our cocks and said, "I'm doing this because I saw
you with your hands down there and I want to make sure you
haven't got a certain disease." '

I remarked that this was probably merely the schoolmaster's
periodical panic about masturbation.

'Tell that to the marines,' said Tom. 'The old boy wanted to
have a feel.'

What I disliked about the Ape, and still dislike to this day so
that, no matter how hard I try to be fair and credit him with
whatever good points he may have possessed, I still feel a strong
wave of resentment amounting almost to fury, was his sardonic
philistinism. He was a congenital enemy of the artist and the
intellectual. Any boy who showed originality he would pounce
on and try to wither with heavy sarcasm. He wasn't stupid; his
comments on the Saxon characters in *Ivanhoe* and on some of
the Old Testament worthies were often quite entertaining; but
I never learned anything from him. His temper was bad and
his voice when he was enraged would rise to a scream like
that of an angry rhinoceros. 'Go on, walk round!' he would
scream.

'Walking round' was the traditional Mowdenian punishment. It meant what it said: you walked round the perimeter

of the entire grounds, which comprised, I suppose, about seven
acres. Most of the way there were wooden palings with shrubs
and privet bushes, and the only interesting thing was watching
the spiders. One huge spider, with a beautiful mottled fat body,
was christened 'the prisoners' friend' by Binkie Burt (who had
to walk round even more than I did) and me. I didn't have
much to do with the Ape my first term, though, as I will tell
you presently, I did encounter his philistinism in a most
atrocious form.

I think there were about six of us in the bottom form. One
was a day-boy named Webb, with whom for a time I became
very friendly. Another was a rather pathetic looking person
with green-gold hair who just missed having a touch of the elf
about him. His name was Greenwood and I christened him
the Frog, from the French *grenouille*. Another was Chichester.
He was a good-natured lazy boy, a little older than me; there
must have been some coloured blood in him for he was very
dark-skinned. He had a cheerful disposition and I doubt
whether his IQ was very high. Our form mistress, Miss Corn-
ford, was a gentle person with a dark moustache. She taught us
a little Latin and a good deal of pattern-drawing. One evening
a week we did 'reading' with BAS in the library. We read a
rather footling book called *Tommy Smith's Animals*. For scrip-
ture we were taught by the assistant master, Mr McNally, a
dapper Irishman with a grey moustache who smelt strongly of
carnation-scented hair oil and whisky. He used to read the New
Testament with a strange passionate intonation, pronouncing not
only every syllable but almost every letter. I was frightened of
him but rather liked him.

BAS took prayers every morning before breakfast and every
evening before supper, which consisted of milk and biscuits.
On Sundays we wore 'Eton' suits and Eton collars and marched
down a very steep chalk hill to church at Preston. In the afternoon we marched, accompanied by Janet, to St Peter's Church,
Hove for a children's service conducted by Canon Flynn, who

pleased me by reciting from the pulpit in a broad Cork brogue: 'I love little pussy, her coat is so warm, and if I don't hurt her she'll do me no harm.' The food was tolerable, but there were already signs of wartime economizing. Breakfast was porridge, and sometimes only one sardine. Bread was unlimited. Lunch was two-course. Tea consisted of potted meat or sometimes lentils, which I found delicious, bread, and honey or jam. I've often wondered whether this diet was sufficient for growing boys. I know that when my parents came down one afternoon about three weeks after the beginning of this, my first term, and took me out for tea to a 'creamery' in Hove, I ate six poached eggs and three ice creams.

Tom Falkner, dear kind funny Tom Falkner, from Galliwood near Chelmsford, was my link with the older boys. He was three years older than me, not good at games; we often walked to church together. It was Tom who introduced me to Harrison Ainsworth, though not, I think during my first term. I started with *Old St Paul's*. The villainy and lechery of the Restoration rakes, Rochester and Sir Paul Parravicin, alarmed me. I had a strong puritan streak, since much modified, and I sided entirely with the virtuous Leonard Holt. The awful fate of the grocer's beautiful daughter Amabel – whom Tom insisted on pronouncing to rhyme with 'table' – gave me a sharp pang. Chowles, the coffin-maker, frightened me and I was genuinely terrified of Judith Malmayns, the plague nurse. In Cruikshank's illustration she looked a little like my mother. I told my mother this during the holidays and she was delighted. Grotesque resemblances always amused her, even if they were at her own expense: once she took Pat and me to the cinema in Exmouth to see a film of the French Revolution, and was pleased when we insisted that the chief *tricoteuse* looked exactly like her.

Gradually the senior boys came into focus. There was a very dashing dark boy called Barson, of whom I was instinctively frightened, though he never spoke to me. He was one of the

Ape's pets. There was also a dark-haired boy with a rather haughty face named Tufnell. He too came from Essex. The difference between a quite senior boy and a junior boy during one's first term at prep school may not be quite so marked as the equivalent difference between a fifteen-year-old and a head prefect – whom one might easily mistake for a master – at a public school; but it's quite noticeable. At Mowden very senior boys – perhaps half a dozen – wore long trousers. Another obvious natural distinction, to be spotted during the communal shower baths after games, is the senior's pubic hair. The transition and the changes in social status that goes with them from new boy to junior to senior are curiously similar at both prep schools and public schools. That, anyway, was my experience. In fact, I'm not sure that, unless puberty is very long delayed, the difference between a boy of nine and a boy of fourteen isn't relatively greater than the difference between a boy of fourteen and a boy of eighteen. These rates of change are difficult to measure, accompanied as they are by sudden fits and starts, moral points.

It was a fine hot summer. We played a little cricket, which bored me. We also each had a garden, a tiny patch. I was no gardener, though in very early childhood I had had a passion for flowers, and my Governess, Miss Clarke, who came after Nanny Skinner left and with whom I was for a time in love, told me that after buying some seeds I kept saying in my sleep: 'Marigolds, marigolds.' This passion for flowers was partly engendered by reading a delightful book by Maurice Baring about a ball which the flowers gave. The two lovers were the Tiger Lily and the Rose. There was a delicious Edwardian illustration of them in a boat on the lake; the Rose was in a swoon of delight and the Tiger Lily was bending over her. I remember at Mowden several of us going with Janet to a nursery garden some way up the Dyke Road and buying seeds. The garden was shady and exciting, but incomplete in my eyes because by this time my love of reptiles was so strong that my

ideal landscape was the frontispiece to the volume on Reptiles
in the Rev. J. G. Wood's *Natural History*: a marvellous jungle
pool with every imaginable snake and lizard disporting
themselves.

When it rained I was delighted because that meant no games
and I could read in the library. During my first term I read
Sherlock Holmes, some school stories, and Anstey's *Vice Versa*.
I was convinced that this must have been written about a real
prep school. The transformation or metamorphosis of Mr
Bultitude into the body of his son, Dick, I allowed to be
fantasy, but Dr Grimstone seemed only a rather caricatured
version of BAS, and the feeling of fear and doom which,
though farcical, was yet quite palpable, was exactly the same
as I experienced at Mowden. And being myself rather pompous
and precocious, always eager to identify with grown-ups, I
found it very easy to identify with the unfortunate Mr
Bultitude.

What else did I read? I remember very distinctly one book
about a boy who was adopted by a country squire and christened Dexter by the doctor because of his manual dexterity.
Nothing went right for this boy. When he went fishing, and
he and a friend were cooking the fish over a wood fire, the
friend fobbed him off with a chub and himself ate the delicious
trout which Dexter had caught, on the pretext that its tail was
burnt. As I was always hungry, any incident about food stayed
in my mind. Dexter, though by the end of the story beginning
to find himself, was obviously in for a long haul. I've often
wondered why this book left such a vivid impression on me. I
think, now, that I was myself suffering from some sense of
incomplete identity. I know that during my first term I several
times had the quite common fantasy that my parents weren't
my real parents but guardians for real parents of immense
distinction.

The head of the school was a boy named Hatchell. He was tall, with tight curly hair, the kind of dark brown curly hair that reminds me of pubic hair. He was going to Haileybury next term. The Snells, being both Haileyburians, had a strong connection with this to my mind rather dour school. His principal duties as head of the school consisted of getting up early and ringing the bell. He was quiet, rather nice, I thought . . . but wait a minute.

One morning, about three weeks after the beginning of my first term, when I had got over the early homesickness and anyway was looking forward to my parents' coming down to take me out, the great Chichester row exploded. Chichester, perhaps on account of being partly coloured, was almost the only one of us who had any knowledge of the notorious facts of life. I don't think any of the rest of us had been given any sexual instruction whatever. Well, Chichester wrote in a notebook a little sexual saga about the marital life of BAS and Ma BAS. We never saw it, but the rumour was that it went something like this: 'Old Man BAS has a Thing three hundred yards long. Ma BAS has a hairy hole three hundreds yards deep. Old Man BAS puts his thing into Ma BAS's hairy hole' . . . and so on. Chichester must have dropped this notebook. Hatchell picked it up just before prayers and took it to BAS. I suppose that he himself was horrified by it.

Today any normal self-respecting married man would take such an overestimation of his potency as a compliment, but not BAS. We had just started breakfast when he rushed into the room with a roar of 'Chichester!' He seized him by the collar of his grey flannel jacket and dragged him from his chair and out of the room with his legs trailing behind him, leaving the door open. Our table, presided over by Janet, was nearest the door. Janet got up and shut it. I said: 'Miss Snell, what's Chichester done?' Janet told me to go on with my breakfast. Presently the door opened again and BAS reappeared, grey-faced. He said: 'I have given Chichester the severest thrashing I have ever given any boy in my school, for unspeakable filth

and beastliness. Chichester will be in silence for three days.'
(I have a feeling he said three weeks but this cannot have been
so; anyway, I'm pretty sure that in effect the silence only lasted
three days.) 'During that time anyone found talking to him
will be most severely punished.' BAS didn't go to the head of
the sixth form table where he usually sat; presumably he had
no appetite for breakfast. I looked at the middle table where
Ma BAS and the Ape always sat with, from time to time, one
or two of the few day-boys. They weren't speaking. I gazed
around the diningroom. Almost above my head was an engrav-
ing of an illustration to Kipling's story 'The Drums of the Fore
and Aft' which depicted Jaikin and Lew, the two little drummer
boys, marching forward in their attempt to stop the rot that had
overtaken their regiment. I also looked at the photographs of
past Mowdenians all along the walls. There was one boy in
particular who had nicely brushed fair hair and a rather sophis-
ticated-looking face; I was always interested in him; Janet
did once tell me who he was and where he went but I've
forgotten.

I don't think I felt at the time any sense of outrage at the
flogging of Chichester. A school row in which one is oneself
guiltless always produces a feeling of selfish cosiness that is
really rather hideous. *Suave mari magno.* . . . The details of
Chichester's crime was all over the school between the end of
breakfast and the first lesson. How did I react? I think, though
it's difficult to be certain, with a split. One part of me was
titillated and almost relieved by Chichester's cheerful Rabelai-
sian fantasy. And, though I was officially ignorant of the 'facts
of life', I certainly didn't feel any of the trauma that is supposed
to go with a too crude initiation. My puritan side was mildly
shocked. There was some repressive element at work, for my
curiosity, which must in fact have been stimulated, was kept in
check. Anyway, we first-termers were far too timorous to dis-
cuss it among ourselves. By lunch time a curtain of silence had
come down.

BAS seldom flogged boys though he quite often hand-strapped them. He used a punishment-strap or tawse, as they call it in Scotland, supplied by the Educational Supply Association. His method of flogging was to take the boy up to his own private bathroom, make him take his trousers and pants down and bend over the bath. This was traditionally known in the school as a bottying. A very severe one was called a blue bottying. Chichester's must have been the bluest in the history of the school: I can't remember when he reappeared but it wasn't for some time, and when he did join us in class he was still in tears. For the three days all his free time, when he would otherwise have been out in the playing field, was spent walking round. We didn't dare speak to him in public but in the dormitory we spoke to him furtively. He showed us his bottom and I can remember plainly the blue welts on his brown skin. He said BAS was in such a rage that he thought he was going to have a fit. He couldn't remember how many strokes he had been given. In fact, as I learned many years later, it was poor Chichester himself who had a fit – it seems he suffered from some sort of epileptic condition. He left long before I did.

My parents came down for the afternoon and I ate six poached eggs and three ice-creams. Tom Falkner came out too. His father was now at the front in France. Neither of us, naturally, said anything about the Chichester bottying. After my parents went back to Blackheath I had another sharp attack of homesickness but it didn't last long because I knew they were coming down for half-term.

Half-term was the usual occasion with no work and a parents' match. On the Saturday morning there were sports and to my great surprise I broke nearly all the school records for boys under nine. I was furious because we were presented with little bronze medals instead of prizes, as a war-time economy. This reminded me of an occasion when, aged three, I was taken by Nanny Skinner to a garden party in Essex and ran in a race.

There was a table loaded with glittering prizes. I toddled up to a man in a panama hat and said: 'Where's my prize?' He explained that I hadn't won the race. I burst into tears and rushed to Nanny Skinner for consolation, which she provided because she was always too inclined to indulge my delusions of grandeur. Once, after having been taken to Galliwood Races, I lolloped up to her in imitation of the gait of a racehorse and said: 'Nanny, I can run as fast as a racehorse can't I?' – 'Well, nearly, dear,' said Nanny.

On the Saturday afternoon, after a special lunch with veal and ham pie and ice-cream, there was the parents' match. There was a shortage of parents because so many fathers were away at the war. My father, who was then touching sixty, agreed to play. I was quite sure he was going to do something tremendous and I watched spellbound as he did a little fielding practice with another parent. He wore, as he nearly always did for the rest of his life, a striped blue suit and a two-inch double-stiff collar with a spotted bow tie. I was disappointed when he didn't bowl – he had once told me he was by way of being a roundarm bowler – and when he went in to bat last. The other batsman was run out before my father had taken the bowling. Were either of Chichester's parents there? I'm not sure but I have a hazy recollection that Mr Chichester was around, a big man with a moustache. Mrs Snell was all smiles on all sides, beaming like a lighthouse. The Ape, in his Jesus blazer and white trousers, cracked jokes.

I went into Brighton by tram with my parents who were staying at the Royal Crescent Hotel, had dinner and caught a tram back and was in bed by nine.

Next morning I arrived at the Royal Crescent for breakfast. My mother was still in bed. My father said she had a headache. She was very piano all that week-end and I wonder now if she mightn't have been having the menopause. After breakfast my father and I walked to the Palace Pier. Just before we got there I said: 'Daddy, how are babies born? Is it the same as with

whales and sharks?' My father said I was too young to be concerned with that sort of thing. I think now that I resented this
brush-off bitterly though I can't remember feeling any very
strong emotion at the time; no doubt because I already knew
most of the answer to my own question. It was a beautiful blue
June day. The sea was dancing and the houses eastward of the
Palace Pier looked, as they always do, like a dream. After lunch
we drove to Rottingdean for tea in an open horse-carriage.
The driver was very old and his horse even older. He, the
horse, started farting and I counted seventy-six farts, very noisy
and smelly ones, between Black Rock and Rottingdean. It was
a rather gloomy outing in spite of the weather and I felt out of
contact with my parents.

I suffered more pangs of homesickness for the next few days
but, as dear Tom Falkner pointed out, the term was now more
than half over and the summer holidays would last for eight
weeks. Tom and Chichester and I and another boy named
Chaplin, who was lame and didn't play games, began to make
pots from some clay we dug up in our gardens. I, being rather
clumsy fingered, wasn't much good at it but I enjoyed it. The
masterpiece, for which Tom and Chichester were chiefly responsible, was a teapot with for a spout a hollow thistle stalk.
We were so proud of this and some of the pots that we asked
the aged boot-boy if he would bake them for us in his furnace.
Near the gardens at the back of the house, surrounded by sad
laurels, was the cess-pit. Once a week BAS could be seen pumping this, working a gigantic iron handle.

'I hope the stink chokes the old beast,' whispered Tom.

'So do I,' said Chichester.

The boot-boy baked our pottery and two afternoons later we
were proudly inspecting it when suddenly behind us we heard
the voice of the Ape. 'What's all this? You're not supposed to
be mucking about. You're supposed to be playing cricket. Go
on. All walk round, the lot of you!' And he stamped our pots
flat.

Even now I cannot recall this act of brutal wanton philistinism without feeling furiously angry. To discourage small
boys from any creative endeavour is criminal. Later on I saw
much more of the Ape, generally to my cost in suffering and
anxiety, and looking back on what I then observed, I now
think he was a frightened man. I remember him saying to me,
when I'd been reading Kipling's *Stalky and Co.*: 'I wish my
brother wouldn't allow that rotten book to be in the library.
It puts silly ideas into boys' heads.' Perhaps he lived in fear of
an *émeute*, a sudden outburst of anarchy, a revolution. How easy
it would be, theoretically, for forty-five or even twenty determined boys to smash up a prep school.

The term wound on. At last there was only a fortnight left.
I began to feel uppish. Someone had been given a veal and ham
pie which was shared out at our table for tea. I turned on the
poor little Grenouille and said: 'Give me yours this instant.'
He handed me his plate. Janet intervened at once and spoke to
me sharply. A few evenings later, when we were reading in the
library, as there was no one to take us as a form, I had a sudden
fit of wild euphoria. I lay on the bench of the desk at which I
was sitting and kicked my legs in the air. I said repeatedly:
'I'm feeling frightfully bucked.' Someone – I think and hope
it was Chichester for I'd like to feel that he had recovered some
spirit – told me to shut up and stop making a nuisance of
myself.

The only other event of any note was the disappearance of
Mr MacNally. He got wildly drunk one Sunday and somebody
told BAS he was behaving strangely. I think he left that very
evening.

The last morning arrived and I drove in a taxi with some
others down to Brighton Station in a haze of joy. My Aunt
Puck met me at London Bridge and we drove to Waterloo in a
hansom cab, the first of many such journeys. Puck used to tell
me afterwards that at Waterloo I would invariably disappear
into the lavatory and stay there so long that she began to fear I

had had a fit or been kidnapped. She put me in charge of the guard on the train for Budleigh Salterton where my parents had taken a house for the summer. The train-journey was a continuous glow.

3

The house was in Links Road and belonged to an old lady, Mrs Theobald, whose grandson, Sonny Fraser – his real christian name was Hillam – I had met during the Easter holidays. He had taken me fishing in the eel pond near the mouth of the river Otter and had caught, to my intense envy, a large eel. Both his parents were dead and he and his two younger sisters, Marjorie and Alison, lived with their Aunt and Uncle, Mr and Mrs Sam Baker. Sam was the local solicitor, a foxy looking fellow who used to go to the saloon bar of the Feathers when he left his office. His wife was a doer of good works and a local magistrate. I don't think they were a well matched couple. Sonny once told me they'd go for days without speaking a word.

The house was small and semi-detached. The garden at the back gave on to a wood and a thicket of gorse bushes. I dug a gigantic hole in this wood, helped by a friendly chap named Spargo who was on leave from Mesopotamia and wore a light tropical uniform. I think he was courting a house-parlourmaid my parents had brought down from Blackheath. My parents played golf. My sister Pat went around with various girl-friends. I saw a good deal of Sonny Fraser, who was three or four years older than I was and a naval cadet at Osborne. I bathed a lot but I don't think it was until the next summer that my father taught me to swim. My favourite occupation was catching lizards. At the bottom of Links Road was a small common covered then with thick heather and gorse, all of which has now been uprooted. At the edge of this common, farthest away from the road, was a pine wood bounded by a sloping bank: ideal lizard-hunting country. The common lizard – *Lacerta vivipera* – suns itself on clumps of heather and gorse. On the top of the bank I quite often found slow-worms – *Anguis fragelis* – those pretty brown legless lizards which are great slug-eaters. Inside the wood were little patches of heathery under-growth, and here, for some reason, the lizards were almost green (*L. vivipera* varies enormously in colour). I used to walk very slowly all the way along the bank which sloped downhill sharply towards the north. I don't suppose I walked more than a few feet a minute. Then I would walk back on top of the bank for part of the way, and then draw the edge of the wood. On a sunny day I generally got two or three lizards. I didn't keep them all, only the best and largest specimens. They are beautiful little creatures with their elegant spidery claws and sharp heads. The young are dark bronze; as they grow up, which they must do fairly fast as I seldom saw an intermediate-sized specimen, their colour changes completely. I preferred the males with their orange and black spotted bellies to the females with their ochre bellies, although this shade of ochre is exquisite. These lizards are hard to catch intact as their tails are very fragile and can break off almost as if at will. The broken end of the tail hops madly – I am sure this must have survival value, the skipping fragment being able to distract predators. My method was to make a sudden grab, getting my hand right round the lizard and the tuft on which it was sitting. I would then extricate the lizard very carefully from the tuft, quite regardless of gorse pricks. They struggle furiously and bite at first, but become docile in a few minutes. When a lizard loses its tail it grows another quite quickly, but the new tail never has the same fine elegance as the old. Slow-worms also have this tail-losing trick and need to be grabbed carefully and firmly high up the body. They too wriggle furiously and have a tiresome habit of shitting on one's fingers. They also become docile in a few minutes and seem quite to enjoy being handled.

I knew from the Reverend J. G. Wood that there were no sand-lizards in Devonshire. The distribution of the sand-lizard is confined to parts of Dorset, Hampshire, and Surrey, and for

some reason to a certain sandy heath near Southport in Lanca-
shire. This is a splendid lizard, *Lacerta agilis*, bigger and sturdier
than the common lizard; the males in the breeding season are
lovely creatures with purple and green sides and backs. The
Rev. J. G. Wood maintained that sand-lizards languish in cap-
tivity. They are not easy to keep but the Belgian herpetologist,
Rollinat, has kept sand-lizards successfully, and inclines to credit
them with high intelligence. Their mating activities include
elaborate nipping and nosing which can be described without
too much imagination and anthropomorphism as love-play. I
didn't know any of this at the time or I would have yearned for
a sand-lizard.

I knew there were adders on this common because I had seen
one during the Easter holidays when I was sitting in a small oak-
tree sucking at a stem with an oak apple on it, pretending it was
an opium pipe. One hot sultry afternoon in August when the
sky was overcast I was walking along the bank looking for
lizards. I had with me a huge ash-stick which I had cut from a
hedge. Suddenly I saw a large brown adder stretched out almost
at full length on an open patch of dark grey sandy earth. I stood
transfixed for several seconds. Three dragonflies shimmered
past; this bank was also very rich in insect life. I was trembling
with a mixture of excitement and fear. The adder was an enemy
(my attitude to adders changed abruptly later after reading
W. H. Hudson). I raised my stick high above my head with
both hands and brought it down with a tremendous thwack on
the adder's back. I hit so hard that it flew up into the air and fell
at my feet, on a clear patch of grass at the foot of the bank. It
writhed about and hissed. There was a kink in its back where
the stick had caught it and beads of blood oozed through the
broken skin. It could move its head and wriggle its tail but its
back was broken and there was no coordination between the
two ends of its body. I poked it with my stick and it gave a
shrill pinging hiss. Suddenly it lifted its head and gaped its
mouth wide open. Something dark and glistening with slime

came out of its pearly mouth. It was the body of a fieldmouse, recently swallowed, with every hair intact. I was surprised that the adder with its tiny head could have swallowed so fat a mouse.

I hit the adder once more and it lay still. Thunder rumbled and heavy drops of rain began to fall. I carried the adder home on my stick. My mother had just come back from playing golf and I showed it to her. She said I mustn't touch it. I said I wanted to skin it. She said, no, but she would ask Brooks the caddy master, an odd half-gypsy man with a stone-bald head, if he would skin it for me. Next day Brooks refused point blank, so the adder was buried in the wood at the back of the house.

In September I had a lucky find. I overturned a stone and collected a whole brood of young slow-worms. The young slow-worms are very different from the mature ones. They are lighter in colour and far more serpentine in their movements as compared to their parents, who are rather stiff. I kept them under a meat-safe. All my lizards were released before we went back to Blackheath at the end of the holidays; but this didn't give me any severe pang as I knew that I'd be able to catch many more next Easter.

I don't remember much else about those holidays. Once I had an attack of rage with Sonny Fraser. He threw me to the ground and when I got up I hurled croquet balls at his head. My sister Pat arrived at this point and I calmed down. Sonny was very good-natured about it. We played a certain amount with two brothers named Reason. The elder was called Bobbity because of his walk. He was, I should think, a budding intellectual being old for his age and having a lofty pedantic manner like a Victorian clergyman. His manner was sardonic rather than sarcastic; he always spoke in grave measured tones. He was very resourceful. He made stilts which I could never master. My birthday present from my mother at my special request was an axe. I must have been in an aggressive mood.

The war had had very little impact on me since it began two years before. My half-brother Wilfred who was a professional soldier, a captain in the DCLI, had been taken prisoner in August 1914 and reported 'wounded, missing, believed killed'. In October 1914, my father got a letter from a nun who had nursed him to say that he was alive. My sister and I celebrated by beating on teatrays. My aunt ran a stall with cups of tea for soldiers on the heath. Later, she ran a home for Belgian refugees. For Christmas 1915 my father carved the turkey; he was a brilliant carver and managed to make one turkey go round some fifty Belgian refugees. The slices must have been as thin as if they had been cut with a microtome, and my aunt said that some of the refugees complained that they would have been better fed under the German occupation.

On a blue winter evening, coming home from a walk, I heard a newsboy shouting 'Great Russian Victory'. My father sent me off to buy a paper. In Budleigh Salterton the war was more remote. The chief activity to which the Saltertonian ladies devoted themselves was picking sphagnum moss on Woodbury Common for wound-dressings.

The world of the young grown-ups was beginning already to fascinate me. At the bathing place on the front, where there were still old-fashioned bathing machines on wheels, the acknowledged queen was Mildred Fulton. She was very tall with a beautiful figure and looked terrific in her bathing-dress with long black stockings. I admired her diving from the little white raft which Gooding, the bathing-beach man, used to moor a few yards from sea.

And one afternoon when we went for a picnic with the Frasers to the Chine, I saw something even more interesting. Sonny Fraser's eldest sister Betty was there on leave from being a VAD. There was a young officer in the FCR on ten days' leave from France. Climbing about by myself on the slopes of the Chine I came across them clasped in each other's arms, and retreated startled and rather shocked. I don't remember this young man's name but I do remember that he was killed flying a few weeks after he got back to France.

4

The autumn of Michaelmas term, which is the true beginning of each school year, is a sad confusing season. When it starts the evenings are still light and the days still warm. On the way to school in the train you see people playing tennis while the leaves are already falling and everything combines to give you a faint yet distinct sense of disorientation. A friend of mine at Oundle wrote in his diary: 'The winter term begins on the hottest day of the year'.

Arriving back at Mowden I wasn't quite so homesick as the term before. There were several new boys, among them the irrepressible Binky Burt, and Ovens. Binky, sometimes known as Trub, which is his name spelt backwards, was an intelligent, imaginative and ugly boy with greenish hair and a large loose mouth. He was the son of a planter from Java, brought up fairly rich, lived in London and had been with his elder sister to lots of musical comedies. Ovens was small and square with huge violet eyes; he was a very firm character, scientific by temperament; he afterwards became the chief medical officer in a West Indian island and I read a long appreciative obituary of him in the British Medical Journal a few years ago.

Janet had invested in a new dog, a black Aberdeen puppy, who licked my face and smelt delicious. I don't think he survived long but he got on quite well with BAS's elderly Dachshund, Scamp. Tom Falkner always called the soup we had during the morning break 'Scamp Soup' and maintained that Janet made it by dipping Scamp's tail in hot water.

The first item on the agenda was the general knowledge paper which was done by the entire school and marked by BAS. The idea was that you did this paper off your own bat and then took it home at the end of the term and got your parents to help you. I can only remember one question which was 'What are the Chiltern Hundreds?' To my astonishment when the marks were put up on the notice board I found I was top in the entire school. I was gazing at my name when the Ape shambled up. 'Don't go thinking, Richardson, that that means anything. What counts is how you do next term when you've had time to work on it at home.' This was characteristically Apeish.

There was also a new assistant master, a rather good-looking tall dark young man, Richard Lee. He took the second form into which I'd moved up. I liked Mr Lee. He was rather self-conscious at times but friendly and quite funny. Sometimes we used to stand behind him when he sat at his desk and we would queue up with our exercise books; we would notice traces of yellowish hair oil at the ends of his rather long black hair and giggle at each other and wonder what it would taste like. He set out by being very conscientious and wrote out careful 'characters' of the first eleven. (We played soccer in the autumn term and rugger in the spring term.) He pinned these characters on the notice board but for some reason the Ape disapproved and they were taken down almost immediately. I rather enjoyed that term and came out top of my form with particular good marks in Latin and in English. Burt who was, I think, two months older than me, was second.

For the holidays I went back to Colonnade House, Blackheath. I had a room at the top of the house; there were some of my own books and also some belonging to the house, including an adventure story about the Navajo Indians which had a wild and melancholy twist to it. I read it when the wind was howling in the chimney. The name Navajo had a powerful spell for me though I pronounced it to rhyme with 'lavajoe'.

At Colonnade House one was rather more conscious of the war. On the same floor there was a young lieutenant Mackie with a rather pretty wife, a bit older than him, with sherry-coloured hair and a good deal of make-up. I once peeped into their room when they were out and inspected her dressing-table. He had some job at Woolwich. There was also an elderly dugout major named Usborne who wore an eyeglass and called all women 'dear lady'. My half-sister Mary, who was twenty-five years older than me, told me very shyly, years later, that he had tried to hold her hand during an air raid. There were some air raids that winter, zeppelin raids, and there was an anti-aircraft gun mounted on the heath quite close by. One night of those winter holidays I was woken by the gun. My mother came and fetched me down and we stood outside the house and watched the zeppelin, which looked like a pale cigar trapped in the searchlights. Suddenly there was a little red glow at one end of it and the next moment it was a mass of flames. We all cheered. I think this was the one that was shot down by Lieutenant Robinson. It must have been the same winter that the great Silvertown explosion happened. My father and mother and I had just finished tea in our sittingroom when, without any warning, all the glass of the big regency windows fell outwards and the curtains streamed into the open air. My father jumped to his feet and then fell back into another armchair. My mother said: 'My God, they've got him!' My father said: 'My dear girl, don't be absurd.' Then came the noise of the explosion and then we saw a huge flickering yellow tongue of flame. This was from a gasometer near the TNT factory; its plates had buckled as a result of the blast and the gas caught fire. That gave Colonnade House plenty to talk about.

The proprietress of Colonnade House was a very determined lady, Mrs Japp. Her husband, who reminded me of a moustached version of Chowles, the coffin-maker in *Old St Pauls*, was an air raid warden. On the nights when he had been on duty he turned up at breakfast in a grey dressing-gown, which was considered a dreadful lapse. Mrs Japp had two daughters, Helen and Sheila. Helen was grown up, very friendly and nice to everybody. She liked to sing a popular song of the time:

O Hell, O Hell, O Helen you're divine.

Sheila was about thirteen, the same age as my sister, with whom she had a rather stormy friendship. She was very pretty with brown hair and blue eyes and a retroussé nose. I fell hopelessly in love with her for a time and she once kissed me. She had the most beautiful rounded handwriting, very even and well formed; she showed me an essay which she had written about Chivalry. It made me despair of my own handwriting which varied in slant and size. I was already an obsessional fountain pen fetichist, always trying to experiment with new nibs. Helen, during another air raid when we were all downstairs in the dark, gave me my first cigarette, a De Reszke. Sheila was a great organizer of theatricals; she did a version of *Macbeth* in which Pat played Lady Macbeth and I Banquo, and another of *Oliver Twist* in which she was the Artful Dodger and I Oliver.

Sometimes I used to be taken to the cinema by a Blackheath girl who had worked for my aunt, a cheerful cockney named Louisa. I was very fond of Louisa and always felt uninhibited and gay when with her. Once she farted loudly and giggled merrily which pleased me very much. The most memorable film we went to see was that classic Italian epic, *Cabiria*, made in 1913 with a scenario by D'Annunzio. I believe it was in advance of some of the Griffiths Hollywood epics that came later. The story was about a Roman family living in Sicily. There was an eruption of Etna and to give you the sense of calamity they showed a close-up of two jars on a shelf. The jars began first to quiver, then to tremble, and then to shake madly. The effect was quite terrifying. I've read about this sequence since in histories of the cinema. The giant slave, Maciste, played by a professional strong man, Elmo Armstrong, swam out to sea with the daughter of his Roman master clutched by her dress between his teeth. They were picked up by a Carthaginian galley and taken to Carthage where Maciste just managed to save Cabiria from being sacrificed to Moloch. Later, we saw Hannibal crossing the Alps. This film ran for very nearly three hours in the cinema at Lewisham, and I enjoyed it probably more than any other film I've ever seen.

At Christmas I bought an owl-shaped flashlight which I pinned to my cap; the battery worked from my pocket. It was considered rather eccentric. To this period, too, belonged my first bicycle and my first air-rifle. My father gave me the bicycle and taught me to ride it, pleasing me very much by telling me that the sensation was probably as near to flying as you could get. The air-rifle was nearly disastrous. I shot at birds in the garden of Colonnade House and hit a tom-tit in the eye. This saddened me and in a mood of strange lunacy I decided to fire at human targets. From my bedroom window I shot at an old lady who was bending down near the pond. I hit her on – rather than in – the backside; I'm pretty sure the little lead pellet just bounced off. She started up, clapped her hand to her bottom and looked round. I ducked down below the window-sill. My next target was a greengrocer's boy. I hit him in the neck. He looked up and saw me. My mother rushed upstairs and hauled me down. She dug the slug out of his neck and put a plaster on it for him. I, in tears, apologized most humbly. The boy was exceedingly nice about it and said of course he knew it was an accident. I, lying, said of course I hadn't meant to shoot at him. The gun was taken away but it never occurred to anybody that I had in fact been deliberately shooting at people.

Two other instances of self-destructive behaviour belong to this period. I went down on all fours when Sandy the bulldog was eating his dinner from his trough and crawled over and growled at him. The shock was too much for Sandy, the gentlest and sweetest of dogs; he snapped at me and one of his teeth just caught my upper lip; my mother spoke to him severely but told me I was a little fool and had asked for it. The other occasion was one morning in my bedroom when I looked in the looking-glass and took a sudden dislike to my red face, sticking-out ears, and especially to my hair which was cut in a kind of fringe. I got a pair of nail-scissors and tried to cut my hair, with hopeless results. I slapped myself furiously on the face and then I went out to get the damage repaired. I sat in an agony of embarassment; the barber said in a chummy way: 'It looks as if the rats have been at it.'

Another diversion in Blackheath was going to see my three aunts, my father's sisters, Ella, Alice, and Maud. They lived at 61, Shooters Hill Road, in the house where the mad dwarf had reigned. There were lots of interesting things, some African weapons, a bust of the Emperor Marcus Aurelius for whom I conceived an immediate admiration although I then knew little or nothing about his stoical philosophy, which now has some appeal for me. There was also a set of ivory teetotums and a lot of fascinating animal pictures. Aunt Ella, who was also my god-mother, was a gentle person, kind and affectionate. Alice was what Aunt Puck and my mother called a regular Richardson. She was tall and dark with a slight moustache and was very incisive and domineering. She talked very fast and I think she was highly intelligent although she never used her intelligence anywhere except at the bridge-table where she was known as 'The Scourge'. Maud, the youngest, was another tremendous talker but not so interesting or commanding as Alice who would transfix me with fierce eyes and say: 'I hope you're mathematical; I can't bear unmathematical people.' Perhaps she was thinking of her dead elder brother, poor Guilford. In fact, though not quite a mathematical dunce and occasionally given to doing enormous sums by myself, I was much weaker at maths than at any other parts of my work, and it was this weakness combined with laziness and lack of application which, later on, made me decide to abandon the idea of becoming a scientist, give up zoology and read English (in which I failed to get a degree).

My father generally took me on Sunday morning walks to

see my aunts and they always produced a gigantic slice of very rich plum cake. Sometimes my father also took me to see my cousin Dorothy, daughter of his younger brother, Raymond, who was staying with her mother in Blackheath. There was a tremendous to-do later, when Dorothy insisted on marrying a Canadian private. Back in Canada after the war, he became a bank manager and all was well. Pat went to stay with Dorothy somewhere in the country and wrote to my mother in a puritan mood, a very rare thing with her, saying: 'Dorothy is rather fast and very vulgar.' My mother read this out to me at breakfast, and laughed for quite a time. Dorothy was a big, good-looking bosomy girl with brown hair and a large, rather fine nose. I remember her at this time as friendly and she had the faculty of treating one as an equal. I saw her years afterwards when she had been living in Canada and had become quiet and matronly.

Once when walking with Dorothy and my father on a Sunday afternoon, I suddenly jumped into the air and came down with my feet in a puddle, splashing both of them. My father was absolutely furious and I don't blame him. He would also sometimes take me to the Blackheath men's club where I would sit in a corner of the billiard room and be given cake while my father held forth. One evening he had a row with a man named Patterson who was exceedingly rude to him. I don't remember what it was about but I do know that I felt desperately uncomfortable, almost for a moment sick.

*   *   *

The summer term of 1917 at Mowden was remarkable for an extraordinary reign of terror. It was organized by three boys in the top form, Tufnell, Neil major, and Piper, Tufnell being the ringleader. They had all been reading the Scarlet Pimpernel novels of Baroness Orczy. Instead of siding with Sir Percy Blakeney and his gang of young bucks, their romantic sympathies were enlisted by the Revolution, and they decided to form themselves into a committee of public safety. Now Tufnell was a most intelligent boy – long afterwards, when I told the story to my great friend, the late Professor R. M. Dawkins, he was so impressed that he'd often say: 'I wonder what became of that boy, Tufnell? I'd give anything to know. Couldn't you find out?'

Tufnell realized that if they started a secret society without any specific aim other than general tyranny they would soon get into trouble. What they needed was some kind of high moral purpose that would give them authority and status in the eyes of BAS and Ma BAS and the Ape. The two most obvious policies, which couldn't fail to please, were a crusade against 'beastly talk' and the suppression of ragging, so they announced publicly that they had formed themselves into a council known as 'The Three' which were going to be responsible for the good behaviour of the entire school. They instituted an elaborate system of spies in every form and dormitory. Every morning and every evening, the Three, presided over by Tufnell, met in the gym and received the reports of their spies. Once a week a public meeting of the Three was held in the gym and executions were carried out. It was the custom at Mowden that heads of dormitories were allowed to beat the boys in their dormitories for ragging or any other misdemeanour. Beating was done on the pyjamaed back-side, with house slippers, which had hard and quite heavy heels. It could be quite painful but I don't remember anybody ever getting more than three strokes or perhaps four at the most. I suppose the idea was to turn little boys of from thirteen to fourteen into public school prefects in embryo. Until the reign of the Three there had been no beating apart from the occasional dormitory incident. BAS, Ma BAS and the Ape had an excellent intelligence service; Janet was for ever on the prowl, as part of her duties; they must have known and approved of what was going on. I am pretty sure that the Ape led the chorus of approval. For him the dictatorship of the

Three was a bulwark against the anarchy that he always feared. Also, Tufnell, a good-looking boy from a rather posh Essex family, and a stylish batsman, was one of his pets.

Within a week after the announcement of their *coup d'état*, the Three were in supreme control and everyone went in fear of them. The spies, as soon as their identity became known, had the time of their lives. Portions of jam were piled on their plates; they were made offers of swaps with the balance of trade prodigiously in their favour. And they, in their anxiety to please their masters, sank to unfathomable depths of baseness. During a history lesson I was sitting next to Croft Handley, son of a dentist; I'd always thought of him as rather a friend of mine and he had quite a nice sense of humour. He was asked a question the answer to which was 'John of Gaunt'. I whispered it to him. The next evening, which was execution evening, I was formally charged with 'cheating by helping' and given two, not very hard ones I admit, with a slipper wielded by Piper who used to share with Neil major the duties of executioner. Tufnell sat enthroned on the vaulting-horse. A week or so later I called Croft Handley 'a wretched pick-nose'. For this he reported me to the Three for 'beastly talk'. I got another two. It surprises me now that I ever spoke to him again, but in fact we became quite friendly afterwards.

Never had the school been more orderly, but, as Tom Falkner pointed out, you never knew when you were safe from morning till night. In its miniature way it must have been something like life in Moscow during the Stalin terror. I was now in a big dormitory called Australia. The captain of it was Neil major. I don't think his parents had much money and his brother, a sallow, rather rat-faced boy with a sharp very red nose, once wore a celluloid collar. My parents were coming down for half-term; they had taken rooms somewhere in Brighton near the Hove border. The Neil parents weren't coming. Neil major asked me if I would take them out on the Sunday. It was the last thing in the world I wanted to do but I was too terrified to refuse. My parents gained the impression that the two Neils were my great friends and I think, looking back, I might have been able to detect some surprise on my mother's face. Neil major played up to my father as hard as he could and called him Sir so often that it made me feel slightly sick.

For some reason I always had a great distaste for calling older men Sir unless they were schoolmasters, in which case it was unavoidable. My father used to say: 'They like it and politeness costs nothing.'

To this I used to reply 'I think you're absolutely wrong, Daddy, why should people like to be treated as old?'

It was a fairly miserable occasion for me though the Neils behaved better, on the whole, than I had expected. I think I had been half afraid of some diabolical piece of mockery.

About three weeks after half-term the Three were finding life a little dull so Tufnell decided to stage a gigantic piece of provocation. I suppose he reasoned with himself something on these lines: if we tighten up the reign of terror when everything is so orderly we could be accused of bullying . . . In Australia in the evenings Neil major began muttering against Tufnell. He said didn't we think that Tufnell was getting too stuck up? Wasn't it about time that the Three should be finished? It had been quite a good idea when it started but Tufnell was becoming too much of a good thing. Couldn't we, even, put some poison in his tea? Neil major's acting had been not bad, not bad at all, until this reference to poison. It should have warned me but it didn't. Naturally no more was said about putting poison in Tufnell's tea, but several of us spoke bitterly against Tufnell. Meanwhile, in South Africa, Piper was doing a similar provocation act. Tom Falkner was one of those who fell for it. In Tufnell's own dormitory, India, absolute calm and loyalty prevailed. Soon came the fatal evening when all those who had spoken against Tufnell were summoned to the gym. We were told we had been given a loyalty test. Neil major smirked slyly; so did his brother. Some six or eight of us were given three each with much ceremony.

Tom Falkner said to me on the way up to bed, 'Well we were mugs, weren't we?'

An important part in putting over the provocation, so far as I was concerned, was played by Neil minor. When his brother was out of the dormitory he told us: 'My major is quite serious about this.'

Tufnell was leaving at the end of that summer term, much to everybody's relief. Neil major organised a subscription to give him a present. We all weighed in with a shilling each and he was presented with a copy of *I Will Repay* by Baroness Orczy. He accepted it graciously and announced that the members of the Three for the next year would be Neil major, Piper and Neil minor.

* * *

Those next summer holidays were noticeably ecstatic. My parents had taken another house in Links Road, Budleigh Salterton. Its owner had left us a grey West African parrot to look after, to which my mother became attached. It didn't speak very much apart from croaking at intervals the name Croswell, in a very peremptory tone. Croswell, we discovered, was the owner's parlourmaid. I caught more lizards and had one great excitement. In the wood, just inside the edge, I caught a jet-black lizard, a plump female; she was very lively and had a piece of wireworm hanging out of her mouth at the time. I thought she must belong to some different species altogether and wrote excitedly to the Zoo. They wrote back politely from the reptile house to say that she was almost certainly a 'melanistic variation' of the common lizard; they would be very pleased to accommodate her in the reptile house if I cared to send her along. Unfortunately she escaped in the night; she was one of the liveliest and most characterful specimens of L. *vivipera* I've ever encountered.

A genuinely traumatic incident concerned a fine specimen of a female slow-worm, pregnant. I was playing with her one morning on the little porch outside the front door when I heard a voice behind me: 'What's that you've got there? Do you know that's deadly poisonous?'

It was a great idiot of a greengrocer named Pile who had come to deliver vegetables. Next moment, without any warning, he stamped the life out of my slow-worm with his hobnailed boot.

'See there,' he said pointing to her sharply pointed tail. 'That's the sting, if you was pricked with that you'd be a dead 'un.'

I rushed at him kicking with my sand-shoed feet, shouting: 'You fool, you know nothing, you've killed my slow-worm.'

My mother came out and pacified me and tried to explain that Mr Pile had thought he was acting for the best. I dried my tears and dissected the remains of the slow-worm with a pair of nail scissors. Slow-worms, like the common lizard and the adder, are viviparous and produce their young alive. Inside the body were eight young slow-worms, each in a little membranous sack. They would have been born in a few weeks' time. My sister Pat arrived on the scene at this point and I showed them to her. She made some remark about babies being born. I was faintly alarmed because although I knew quite a lot about animal life I still had some curious blockage so far as human beings were concerned. I don't think the idea of my parents having sexual relations had reached conscious expression.

That summer my father taught me to swim. He did this very thoroughly with a rope and a webbing belt. We were rowed by an old fisherman named Hitt, rather a chum of my father's. It was another hot summer and the sea close under the cliffs by the Rosemullion Hotel was beautifully clear. There was a lot of brown and green seaweed which I looked down at as

I swam. By the end of a week I could swim and from then onwards, all through a succession of summer holidays, I bathed never less than twice a day and sometimes three times. I wasn't taught the crawl, which was a pity because its rhythm takes some learning once you have started swimming either side-stroke or in that over-arm trudgeon style, which comes naturally. I used to like to swim out quite long distances, sometimes half a mile, and stop off at the raft on the way back and dive.

In that house in Links Road I read my first Rider Haggard novel, I think it was called *Queen Sheba's Ring*. There was a beautiful white queen, ruler over a savage desert tribe called the Fung. The English adventurer hero fell madly in love with her and she with him. I was madly in love with her myself and have never forgotten her. The climax came when the hero used his stock of dynamite to blow up a gigantic stone statue the head of which went flying into the air and dropped a mile away, thus fulfilling a tribal prophecy and confounding a local native Prince who was trying to win her himself.

Another feature of those holidays was a boy who lived in the house next door and sang a parody version of Land of Hope and Glory which, of course, became Land of Soap and Water. My sister and I made friends with him and I saw quite a lot of him. He was always known as Pussy. He was two or three years older than me and I was very impressed by his care-free panache. I felt he wouldn't have had any difficulties in dealing with either the Ape or the Three. Once I took him lizard hunting and we caught two splendid slow-worms. They were quite aggressive and snapped at our fingers. 'You could wear these as ear-rings,' Pussy said. He nudged the lobe of his left ear with the slow-worm's nose and it bit the lobe and hung there dangling. I put the other slow-worm to his other ear and it too gripped like a bulldog. Pussy was wearing a grey flannel hat to which he had given an Australian effect by turning up one side and securing it with a burr. The slow-worms hung almost motionless and Pussy walked along wearing these live ear-rings, looking indescribably exotic.

About this time, perhaps to requite him for taking so much trouble teaching me to swim, I used to caddy a certain amount for my father. I found this rather boring and my attention would wander. Once my father was playing with a crusty old retired general named Horniblow when I caught a fine lizard and put it in my pocket. On the fourteenth tee the lizard escaped from me and scuffled across the tee just as Horniblow was about to drive off. He made some crack about my father's tactics for distracting him.

5

At Mowden there was a new assistant master, Sanderson. He was a friend of Lee's, a rather jovial, waggish fellow with a touch of sophistication about him. He was in charge of shooting and this was my strongest point. I was a very good shot indeed although occasionally given to fits of irregularity. Both Lee and Sanderson, we now began to discover, were ardent Christian Scientists and were inclined to make propaganda for their sect. If they saw somebody in class blowing on his chilblains they would say: 'You must forget all about your chilblains and they will go. They are only in the mind.'

The new Three over-reached themselves almost at once. There was no longer any vestige of moral purpose in their reign and about a fortnight after the beginning of the term BAS went into action. I can't remember just what precipitated it and I hadn't suffered myself, but I do remember BAS thundering after prayers, just before breakfast, about: 'disgraceful bullying by Neil major, Piper and Neil minor. They will go up to my bathroom now to receive their thrashing. The rest of you will go into breakfast as usual. Any boy who does not instantly report future occurrences of bullying to me will be severely dealt with for disloyalty to the school.' I can see now the rat-like Neil minor slinking up the stairs to get his bottying. At breakfast we were laughing fit to burst.

So that was the end of the Three. But a more serious individual case of bullying occurred that term in the very form I was in, Form Three. There was a boy named Dove, and never has a boy been more aptly named. A soft gentle creature who often looked as if he were on the verge of tears. He had pale freckled skin and brown tight curly hair. I liked him but found him rather too dovelike. He collected crests and helped me to start a little collection of my own; it soon languished because I couldn't be bothered, but I liked the bright reds and blues and the way you could run your fingers over a crest. I much preferred them to stamps, which I've always thought boring.

Dove had a pink-faced persecutor, a vigorous athletic boy named Godstow who always seemed friendly and good-natured on the surface. His father had, I think, been taken prisoner by the Turks. Presently we noticed that Dove was looking increasingly miserable day by day. There were dark rings under his eyes and he was generally in tears at breakfast. One day somebody asked him what was the matter and he said it was Godstow. Godstow was making him get up early before breakfast and go down with him to the sixth-form room where the radiators were hottest. He would prick him with a compass needle, force him to sit on the hot radiator and even once to take out his penis and put it on the radiator. I simply cannot remember what my own reaction was to this. I think I shared in the general reaction which was one of mixed embarrassment and disbelief, although we didn't have any doubt about Dove's suffering. Somebody surely must have said, 'But why do you let him do it?' If they did Dove answered: 'Because I'm frightened of him.' Anyway, almost immediately after that, perhaps on the same day, Dove went and told BAS. BAS hauled Godstow up to his bathroom and gave him a bottying. Godstow never persecuted Dove again and the incident was forgotten. I have a sort of pseudo-memory that Godstow once said something to me about how sorry he was and he didn't know what had come over him, but I have no certainty of this.

I suppose this type of case, in which a sadist, or someone who suffers from a passing fit of cruelty, finds a victim is not uncommon and not of any very deep significance. But it doesn't do to minimize it. Dove, for at least a week, must have had a horrible experience. What shocks me most in looking back on it is that it should have gone on for so long. Personally, if I were running a school, I should make it a rule that any boy who found himself being bullied in any way by any other boy or boys should instantly blow a whistle. The idea that a certain amount of bullying is inevitable and even to some extent desirable as part of a general toughening-up process is atrocious, but it still lingers.

For me this was a gay, comparatively carefree winter term. I kept out of trouble and I was in my usual state of wild euphoria by the end of it. Oh, that prep school end of term euphoria! Was there ever ecstasy to compare with it? There is a peasant saying: 'The happiest moment of the fiesta is on the eve of it', which certainly applies here.

I remember sitting at tea with Burt, Dalrymple, and Littlehales two days before the end of the term. Dalrymple was a rather whimsical boy with a long gnomish face and a good deal of easy self-assurance; he, I feel now, had no doubts about his own identity. He was rather a favourite with the entire Snell family. Suddenly Dalrymple gave tongue with his own version of the traditional end of term jingle: 'This time next week where shall I be?' His big laugh line was: 'No more beastly Littlehales, pissing into little pails.'

Dalrymple had quite a touch of fantasy. It was a tradition at Mowden that in the ventilator above the sixth form room lived Lar, the God of the Hearth. Dalrymple was first and foremost in organizing sacrifices to Lar. 'It's time we sacrificed,' he would say. 'Who's acceptable? Trub, you ugly brute, Lar wants you.' So we would all set on Burt and hold him in the air or on a desk and tickle him while Dalrymple intoned: 'Oh Lar, we pray thee, accept this little gift.' But why should his rhyme have seemed quite so ecstatically funny? We all laughed, including Dick Littlehales, a fair-haired boy with a fringe, a good-natured 'very normal' boy, who was some cousin of the Snells. And my own laughter became, as it were, transcendent; I passed into an ecstasy so acute that it was literally painful.

I had already had one reunion with my parents that term. The circumstances were a little odd. I was called in by BAS from football practice. He was standing on the terrace outside his study with a telegram in his hand. He read it to me. 'Can Richardson and Father come to London for the night. Will meet the train at 5 p.m. Victoria.' We were naturally baffled by the word 'father'. BAS implied that while he didn't in general approve of sudden jaunts to London he presumed there was some reason for it so would I change and be ready to catch the train with him. Miss Snell had already packed a week-end bag for me. Naturally I was delighted, though a trifle embarrassed at travelling in the company of BAS. Perhaps he himself jumped at the chance of escaping from the school and his brother, the Ape, whom I never thought he liked. He sat opposite me in the train wearing his grey cloth cap and I tried, and I think succeeded, in getting him into conversation about Sherlock Holmes's intellectual abilities. He strongly advised me to read Conan Doyle's historical novels *Sir Nigel* and *The White Company*. I'd already read *Rodney Stone* which, with its partly Sussex and Regency Brighton setting, had seemed very close at hand. BAS himself reminded me a little at times of Professor Moriarty, though I naturally did not dare to tell him this.

At Victoria we were met by my father and the mystery of the telegram was explained. The word Father was a mistake for Falkner. Tom Falkner's father, Newstead, was back from France on sudden week-end leave. It was too late to do anything about it and my father took me off to Blackheath. (Quite soon after this Newstead Falkner was killed.) I stayed at Colonnade House and the next morning my mother took me to the Zoo. I spent as much time as she would allow in the old reptile house, a rather rococo Victorian building which went very well with my ideas as acquired from the Rev. J. G. Wood's

Natural History. We lunched at the Zoo on veal and ham pie and meringues. Soon afterwards I was taken violently short and my mother hustled me into the ladies' lavatory. I arrived back at Mowden in time for prayers, feeling rather embarrassed. BAS made several jocular references to 'little jaunts to London' throughout the term.

That winter was our last at Colonnade House. My mother was getting into a bit of a state about the air raids. She was always inclined to suffer from anxiety, though I would scarcely have classed her as a neurotic. I noticed, much later, that she detested the telephone. If I rang her up with some simple message, perhaps to say that I was going to have lunch at the golf club and play another round, she would show relief: 'Is that you, Lad? What is it? . . . Oh I see, yes, all right then.' She seemed to associate the telephone with bad news only. (She had reason for this at the time of my sister's death but that is a story which is outside the scope of this book.)

We moved to a furnished house in Station Road, Budleigh Salterton. During the next few months we moved three times. The house I liked best was Crewshaye which belonged to Colonel Durnford's sister. Here during the Easter holidays I had my great grass-snake adventure. My sister and a boy of about thirteen, Tam Workman, came back from a picnic in Otterton Park. They had found a pond in a field and had seen several grass-snakes. I was wildly excited. Tam promised to take me there next afternoon and we set off on our bikes. Tam led the way when we got to the field. He picked up a stick after we climbed over the gate. The pond was in a corner with a tall hedgerow along two sides of it. It was an ideal grass-snake site with frogs and newts ready at hand and thick cover as well as good grassy sunning places.

'There they are!' Tam pointed with his stick. There were three grass-snakes entwined in a cluster. I've since discussed this habit of grass-snakes with my friend, Reg Lanworn, the herpetologist at the reptile house of the London Zoo and he

thinks it implies some form of sexual connection. Tam certainly
thought so, for with a shout of 'The swine!' he struck at the
grass-snakes with his stick. One of them fell dead at the foot of
the hedge. Another glided away into the hedge. I caught the
third.

The Scottish puritan fervour that had taken hold of Tam
abated and he was pleased to have found a live snake for me.
This was the first grass-snake I'd ever handled but I recognized
it instantly from the description I'd read. The beautiful black
and gold collar behind the head was unmistakable. We hadn't
anything to put it in so I bicycled back one-handed holding the
grass-snake firmly in my left. After the manner of its species it
let out a fearful stink, something like rotten eggs, from the
glands at the base of its tail but I was completely impervious.
The ride home was made extra dramatic because passing
through Otterton Park, we were chased by hornets who had a
nest in an oak-tree near Clammer Bridge. We out-distanced
them and got home safely. I had an egg for tea and the rest of
the evening passed in an ecstasy as I played with my snake. It
soon became used to being handled and stopped making stinks;
but the smell remained on my hands and when, at my mother's
suggestion, I washed them with some strongly scented soap the
resulting smell was more horrible still. Alas, in the night the
grass-snake escaped from the improvised wooden box in which
I had put it. I didn't then realize what brilliant escapologists
most snakes are. I searched all the hedges in the garden of
Crewshaye in vain. Two years later, I recaptured what I think
may have been the same snake, on the bank at the north end
near a stream. It must have travelled until it found the ideal
spot.

One of the things I liked about Crewshaye was that there was
no gas or electric light in my bedroom. The candles were made
of some very odd wax which gave off quite thick smoke and
smuts when you lit them. My room was in an irregular-shaped
attic at the top of the house. One night when I lit my candle the

smuts hung in the air and looked exactly like black notes of music. There was a set of omnibus volumes in Crewshaye which must have been an all-time record: the entire Waverley Novels of Scott unabridged in four volumes. I can hardly believe it to this day but I know it is true. Each volume weighed a ton and the print was minuscule, almost illegible by candle-light. My father had a passion for Scott but he was defeated by this print. A Victorian novel which brought my father and my mother and me close together was Wilkie Collins's *The Woman in White*. This we found in one of the houses we took in Station Road. I read it first at their suggestion, and then they each re-read it. Count Fosco, the master criminal who was so tenderly affectionate to his white mice and so ruthless to every-body else, delighted me. I've since re-read *The Woman in White* at least four times, the last time in order to write the introduc-tion to the new Everyman Edition.

Did I observe, when I first read it, the peculiar character of Mr Fairlie? I think I merely found him a figure of fun quite subsidiary to Fosco, the wicked baronet, Sir Perceval Style, and the two heroines Laura and Marian. I have since remarked that he must be one of the early examples of an obvious shrieking queer in Victorian fiction. It was strange how for the three of us, my mother, my father, and I, reading this novel almost simultaneously, as we did, formed a bond. Looking back, it seems to me that I was sharing one of their more youthful experiences and that, because of this, I was able to bridge the age gap between us, for both of them were fully old enough, biologically speaking, to have been my grandparents.

Two sporting events took place during these holidays, both of which had the effect of increasing my selfconsciousness which in those days was often apt to be heightened. The first was a race organized by the schoolmaster of the Budleigh Salterton village school. My father had decided to go in for local politics and had been elected chairman of the Budleigh Salterton Urban District Council. (His stories of the Council meetings, where his two chief enemies were a Labour – very right-wing, I should think – fishmonger, and a Liberal retired police inspector, of whom he used to say scornfully that his speciality had been tracking down cases of abortion, were so long and so passionate that my mother used to impose a time limit on them at meals.) As chairman it fell to him to present the prizes. I won the principal race and he presented me with a magnificent fruit knife with a large, curved blade in a wash-leather case. At last I had won that prize which had eluded me ever since the age of three; yet I felt, so strong and so absurd were the class divisions of our provincial life, a slight but distinct tinge of embarrassment, almost of shame, at robbing the deserving proletariat of what should really have been their prize. My father's attitude to working class people in Budleigh Salterton was curiously mixed. He would chat with them, being a naturally friendly and sociable person, on equal terms, and I often heard him telling fishermen, with whom he was especially chummy, sophisticated inside stories of the Stock Exchange of his youth. But I think he used to suffer, as many bourgeois gents are apt to do, from sudden fears of falling back into the poverty from which, as a young man, he had only just escaped. Sunday after Sunday, when he came back from his morning walk, he would tell us at lunch: 'I saw Benoke, you know, that red-haired railway porter, nice chap, always very civil. There he was in his best suit, much better dressed than me, out for a walk with his family, all very well dressed. And very nice too. But what I want to know is: how can the country afford it?'

The other sporting event was at the miniature rifle range in a gravel pit halfway up West Hill. This had some very remote connection with the war; I suppose those who used it could be vaguely compared to the Home Guard in World War Two. My father, who was always conscientious in trying to find things for me to do, took me up there one summer evening and handed me over to the gentle, dreamy old buffer with a clipped white moustache, stained brown with nicotine under the nostrils, who was in charge. The shooters were of all classes, all between the ages of fifty and seventy. I, with my Mowden .22 training, was a star performer. Here again I felt that I was somehow competing unfairly, though this time with the aged.

6

The summer term of 1917 began quietly. I was now in a form
which was taken mainly by the Ape. My Latin was all right.
My translations were well above average; my proses would
pass. I remember North and Hillyard and some of the sentences.
There was one, 'While he was speaking a loud report was
heard', which we used secretly to giggle over, pretending it
referred to a huge fart. The Ape himself was more or less
immune to farting, but BAS was obsessed by it. Suddenly he
would pause in front of the blackboard and sniff the air like a
maniacal hound. 'Somebody's made a beast of themselves.'
He'd point with a long witch doctor's finger all round the class.
'Is it you? Is it you? Is it you? Very well then. All walk round.'
So up we would get and troop round the playing field perimeter once and then resume our places.

My torture with the Ape was maths. He was the most un-
imaginative teacher I've ever encountered, dead set in his
approach. If one did a sum in any but the prescribed way his
voice would rise to that shrill rhino scream: 'But you've done
it the wrong way!' I sometimes like to think that if I'd been
taught by a genius, who could have given me a feeling for the
magic of numbers and the quasi-mystical aspect of mathe-
matics, I might have cottoned on and become, though never a
mathematician, at any rate proficient enough to follow a
scientific career. One of the most monstrous things the Ape said
to me I shall never forget or forgive. I had to go to his study for
something. He was sitting at his roll-top desk which was full of
cricket balls, with photographs of cricket and football teams all
round the walls of the room and a bookcase full of Wisdens'
almanacs. The Ape looked at me and said: 'You know you're

very dreamy. That's because you're the son of elderly parents.'
Can you imagine anything more likely to undermine a
small boy's selfconfidence? I walked dismally along the corridor feeling, to use a jargon phrase, semi-castrated. What a
bastard!

However, I was saved by my shooting. I got a possible at the
difficult figure target at twenty-five yards on the very day on
which I was in trouble with the Ape over maths. I remember
BAS, who could be human enough when not on a puritan
rampage, showing the Ape my target at his study window. I
think he said something like: 'We must admit that Richardson
can shoot.'

My shooting friend was Webb, a day-boy, dark and rather
lazy. Once, sitting next to him in a geography lesson taken by
Richard Lee, we came to that famous Mexican volcano,
Popacatapetl. 'Pop a cat in a kettle,' whispered Webb, as generations of schoolboys before and since must have whispered.
We went into a suppressed giggling fit of sheer ecstasy. I had
for a time a tiny, unrealized crush on Webb. I nicknamed him
Ilsabel, after the fisherman's wife in the story of the flounder
which I'd read in one of the Andrew Lang Fairy Books, because
he was always discontented. He asked me home to tea one
Sunday. He lived in a red-brick villa quite near the Bird
Museum. We had marrow jam and after tea Webb's father,
who hadn't spoken a word, produced a stereoscopic frame and
a set of photographs of the Russo-Japanese war; we looked at
them for an hour. After this, I got bored with Webb and saw
less and less of him. The peak of our relationship, apart from
Popacatapetl, was when we were both given our shooting eight
ties, silk ties in the Mowden colours, red and black. We were
handed them by Janet.

My parents didn't come down that half-term. I was asked
out by John Strong, who afterwards went to Oundle. His
father was an old party named Sir Vesey Strong, who had been
Lord Mayor of London. He was staying at the Bedford Hotel,

now burnt down rather mysteriously, the most beautiful of the Brighton hotels, where Dickens and Wilkie Collins used to stay. Sir Vesey was a dear old man. He was suffering from cancer of the throat and he showed me the radium plate which he wore. We had a huge breakfast, sat around in the lounge looking at yachting papers, did the West Pier, had a huge lunch. Brighton was packed. Standing on the steps of the Metropole was a dapper Jewish gentleman in a blue striped coat, white trousers and brown and white correspondent shoes, the first I'd ever seen. Someone made a crack about why wasn't he at the war. The war was beginning to impinge a little more by this time. The fathers of some boys had been killed. I remember one, Waters, being sent for to go and see Mrs Snell because a telegram had come from his mother. I expect it was the thought of his father at the front that had prompted Waters, a rather romantic-looking little boy with dark curly hair, to do his exhibitionist act a term or so before. We were having a kind of field day outing on the Downs and Waters suddenly rushed forward shouting: 'Up boys and at 'em!' The sardonic Dalrymple said: 'Waters, you silly little fool, what on earth do you think you're doing?' Waters blushed scarlet.

The submarine campaign was having its effect that summer term. One Sunday Croft Handley said to me when I was complaining of Ape-persecution: 'Don't worry. I shouldn't be a bit surprised if all schools don't close down soon. The food situation is getting very difficult.' He squeezed a spot on his arm and pointed triumphantly to the dark blood. 'But look at that! That's real pre-war blood for you.'

• A peculiarly maddening invention of BAS when the submarine campaign was at its height was his bread economy drive. He would at the end of tea read out the school list and every boy had to tell him the number of pieces of bread he had eaten. Three was considered good; four permissible; but five, six and seven were received with an angry grunt. Often it was 'Richardson?' – 'Six, sir.' Burt held the record with nine. I will say for BAS that he never insisted that a boy should not eat more than any specified number of slices; even so there was a distinct air of intimidation.

*　　*　　*

Not long after half-term came my major traumatic experience. Piper, the ex-member of the Three, had chummed up with me. He lived in Nottingham, and had a rather theatrical bent; he kept a box of powder in his desk which was labelled 'Lily Louloute's blanche'. I, who as a boy had an anti-cosmetic complex, was faintly horrified. Piper and I used to watch first eleven cricket matches lying on our rugs with the rest of the school. We all had score books and were supposed to keep the score, with every ball and run marked. Piper had asked me to stay for part of the summer holidays and pointed out the delights of Nottingham: swimming bath, cinemas, cafés. It sounded rather attractive and I had provisionally accepted. Then came the fatal afternoon.

We were lying on our rugs, watching a particularly boring match. I said I wanted to go to the bog. I suggested that Piper should come with me, have a drink at the fountain in the boot-room next door to the lavatories, and talk to me through the bog doors which were open at the top and bottom. A diabolical sport was to climb on the seat of your own lavatory, reach over the top and pull the chain of the lavatory next door so that it suddenly flushed under the boy who was sitting on the seat. It was this trick that led to the detection of Coverdale, the crypto-coprophile. He was seen furtively licking a piece of paper with which he had just wiped his arse. There was some fuss about this; I think he got a stripe. (A stripe was a blue form very like a cheque, which was given you for bad behaviour. You found it in your desk on Monday morning. For good work you got a star which was pink. Unfairly, stars were distributed in quarters so you needed four pink cheques to make up a whole star. Star,

or stripe, was shown to BAS at breakfast. He would grunt and
go back to his porridge. Too many stripes meant a hand-
strapping.)

Anyway, Piper and I walked off to the bog and Piper sat
down by the drinking fountain and poured himself out a zinc
cup – on a chain – of water. I, who have always been cheerfully
uninhibited about excreting, sat down on my stool, had my
crap, and carried on an animated conversation with Piper. Then
we went back to the match. Half an hour later Piper said he
wanted to go to the bog so I said I'd come with him. I was sitting by the fountain when a boy named Gooch – not Bobby –
came in. He'd been having a music lesson and was changing his
shoes before going out to watch the cricket match. We played
a short game of catch with a cricket ball. Then Piper emerged
and he and I went back to our rugs.

It wasn't so far off the end of the term and I was feeling fairly
euphoric. There were no signs of a cloud in the sky and the
atmosphere in the school seemed calm. But after prayers BAS
announced in a voice of doom: 'The school will remain
behind.' Ma Snell, the Ape, Richard Lee, Sanderson and Janet
filed out. Then BAS began:

'There has been a lot of beastliness and beastly talk in the
school of late. But I only propose to make an example of two
boys. . . .' I thought: I know: Cox and Neill minor. Their
conversation in the dormitory had been pretty obscene of late;
no doubt they'd been overheard by Janet. But BAS went on:
'Those two boys are: Richardson and Piper!'

At such a moment clichés become inevitable. I literally
couldn't believe my ears. I was stunned with surprise and shock.
I felt as if I was falling through a hole in the floor. The rest of
BAS's diatribe came to me in fragments. 'Miss Snell reports that
during the match this afternoon they were absent in the lava-
tory on two separate occasions for quite long periods. . . .
The only interpretation of such behaviour is beastliness. . . .
I intend that beastliness shall be stamped out of my school. . . .

Richardson and Piper will go up to my private bathroom now to receive their thrashing, and be in silence for three days.'

The rest of the school filed out. I went up to Piper who was white and trembling. I said: 'It's absurd. We didn't do anything. We must tell him.'

I went up to BAS and said: 'Sir, we must speak to you, sir. We didn't do anything, honestly we didn't.'

BAS looked at me and said: 'Very well, come into my study and I will hear what you have to say.'

We followed him into his study, which was very civilized in comparison to the Ape's lair, with books all over the walls and some historical prints and a water-colour of Jesus, Cambridge. BAS pulled a green leather armchair round so that its back was towards us and knelt in it with his arms on the back and his hands clasped, almost in an attitude of prayer. I told him exactly what had happened. He asked why we'd been so long and I said because we were talking. He asked Piper if what I said was true and Piper, who was still almost speechless, said yes it was. I repeated that Gooch had come through the bootroom on the way from his music lesson and we'd played a game of catch.

BAS stood up. 'I shall speak to Gooch,' he said. 'Remain outside in the corridor.' He called for Janet and presently Gooch came pattering down the private staircase in his dressing-gown, looking terrified. I whispered quickly: 'Tell him about the game of catch.'

I don't know how long Gooch was in there; it probably wasn't more than five minutes but it seemed a very long time. Piper and I stood silent in the corridor. Gooch came out and scuttled off upstairs to his dormitory. BAS called us in.

'Gooch has corroborated your story,' he said. 'You may go.'

We said: 'Thank you, sir,' and went. I don't think he even said 'goodnight'. He muttered something about: 'You must understand that the bootroom and lavatories are not the places to hang about in, especially when you should be watching cricket.'

When I got back to my dormitory, still Australia, there was a strained silence. Everybody, of course, was dying to ask what the bottying had been like, how many we'd had etc, but at first they were afraid to speak. BAS had been in particularly swingeing form, ending up with an appeal for a crusade to stamp out beastliness for the honour of the school.

I was the first to break the silence. I said: 'It's all right. We hadn't done anything so we were let off.'

'Then you haven't been bottyed?'

'No, of course not.'

'What about the silence?'

'I don't think it's safe to speak to him. Janet might overhear.'

'We're not in silence either.'

'You certain?'

'Yes, absolutely.'

Then the questions began. 'Ooh, I'll bet you were frightened, weren't you?'

'Lucky for you Gooch happened to be having a music lesson.'

For the rest of the term I avoided Piper. I got a letter from my mother saying Mrs Piper had written to ask if I could come to stay during the summer holidays. I wrote back saying I'd changed my mind and didn't want to go.

Rider Haggard had now become my passion. I'd read *King Solomon's Mines* and *Alan Quatermain*, its sequel, and fallen in love with both Queens, the fair one and her dark wicked sister. I'd also read Anthony Hope's *The Prisoner of Zenda* and *Rupert of Hentzau* and was wild about Flavia. That meant being in love with three queens simultaneously. Then I read Rider Haggard's *She* and gave them all up for the immortal Ayesha. I identified with Holly, the ugly strong-man narrator, and was rather jealous of Leo, the incarnation of Kallikrates, She's lover from the past. Like Swinburne, about whom I read later, I despised Leo for not having gone into the Fire of Life first time round and thus spared She her fearful metamorphosis into a woman aged

2,000 years. What a ripe fantasy this is; Freudians and Jungians could hold a joint field day over it.

There was a boy in Australia, Gordon MacGregor, about two years older than me, a gay friendly fellow, who was another She fan. He got so excited that one night he called out 'I've got aromatic fever'. I had a reunion with him in the spring of 1967 when I went to Brighton for a week-end. He went from Mowden to Charterhouse, became a doctor, and is now a flourishing consultant in Hove. We reminisced cheerfully for hours. These reunions are apt to be disappointing but this one was a total success. We discussed the utter absurdity of not giving prep school boys any sex education until the last day of their last term, which was the official Mowden practice.

We weren't allowed newspapers even, with the exception of the *Daily Graphic*, then a very sedate little picture paper; you couldn't call it a tabloid. It had a specially decorative weather report with a line drawing of a Greek goddess. In it I read the first novel of a girl wonder, Molly Panter-Downes, now *The New Yorker's* London correspondent. She was about fifteen, a delicious flapper with a long pigtail and a bow on it. Naturally I fell in love with her. For serious news BAS used to pin extracts from each day's *Times* on the notice board.

We were not only allowed the Bible; it was compulsory that we should have a Bible in our desks. Even at that time I found it difficult to accept the official interpretation of the Song of Solomon as symbolizing not sexual love but love for the Church. Then there were the catalogues of sexual aberrations and their penalties in Leviticus, and the denunciations of the Prophets. I remember reading, during a sermon in the Church at Preston, Ezekiel xxiii: the Whoredoms of Aholah and Aholibah:

'Son of Man, there were two women, the daughters of one mother: And they committed whoredoms in Egypt; they committed whoredoms in their youth; there were their breasts pressed and there they bruised the teats of their virginity.'

My eyes started out of my head and I nearly forgot to stand up at the end of the sermon. For the rest of the day I could think of nothing but the whoredoms of Aholah and Aholibah. I felt a wave of mixed lust and puritanism. I wanted to protect them and avenge their wrongs at the hands of their wicked lovers who had bruised their teats. The official explanation that Aholah and Aholibah symbolized Samaria and Judea didn't begin to register.

7

In the summer a swarm of visitors used to descend on Budleigh Salterton. Most of them were families of the middle and upper-middle classes who had children of school age. They took furnished houses and some of the richer ones stayed in the Rose-mullion or the Rolle Hotel. The war made little difference to this annual invasion; if anything it rather accentuated it because foreign travel was cut off. All this meant that the climate was one of flirtation. Love, in a mild form, was in the air. The gulls cried on the beach and children in paddling drawers screamed at the lap of surprise waves. Hardy old ladies in trailing black silk bathing dresses swam out to the white raft, coiling their withered arms like water-snakes. The air was blue and clear. In the afternoon at the tennis club the leggy, coltish girls made clumsy, sweet, pathetic gestures as they whirled their bare arms round their heads in the attempt to deliver a paralysing service.

For children and adolescents the social centre was Abele Tree House in Fore Street. Here lived the Semples. Dr Henry Semple was one of the Budleigh Salterton general practitioners. He worked hard and you could often see him driving about in an American-looking motor-car. His son, Jack, has since become a highly successful surgeon. The driving force behind Dr Semple was his wife, Charlotte. She was the daughter of a Devonshire clergyman and an indefatigable hostess. For the grown-ups she gave bridge parties and for their children children's parties. Mrs Semple was a short, plump lady with rather wispy hair. She had an inimitable laugh or titter impossible to reproduce but something like: eugh . . . eugh . . . eugh. Her sentences were carefully composed. She said once of her son Hugh, a very likeable, sandy-haired naval officer: 'Hughie's such a butterfly.

Eugh . . . eugh . . eugh. He flits from flower to flower, from girl to girl.' (Hughie later settled for the very rich daughter of a Glasgow hemp manufacturer.) As a hostess, I've often thought that Mrs Semple must have had something in common with Lady Cunard. My parents went to one of her bridge parties and told us afterwards about their hostess's introductions.

'This,' said Mrs Semple, 'is Mr Richardson who has a son who is a prisoner in Germany. And this,' she went on, 'is Mr So-and-So who's son has just been blinded on the Somme. And this' – rising to a crescendo – 'is Mrs Such-and-Such who's husband has just been killed in the war.' Then they all sat down to play bridge.

Mrs Semple's children's parties still remind me of that opening sentence of Alphonse Daudet's: '*Qui n'a pas vu Avignon au temps des Papes n'a rien vu. . . .*' (He who has not been to one of Mrs Semple's children's parties has nowhere been; there you found the provincial *douceur de vivre* left over from the Edwardian era.) The food, a lot of which was cooked by Mrs Semple herself, was fantastic. The ices were unparalleled. I've had many wrangles since with one connoisseur who insists that Gunter's ices between the wars were as good as ices can be, but she never tasted the ices at Mrs Semple's. They were made by Mr Parker, a cadaverous-looking man who kept a baker's and sweet shop and café just opposite Mrs Semple. His secret, in so far as he had one, was simple – fresh fruit and Devonshire cream – but I have never tasted anything like them.*

Mrs Parker used to play the piano in Mrs Semple's drawing-room. She played very slowly except for Sir Roger de Coverley, when her stumpy little fingers jigged merrily over the keys.

* Once, after bathing, my father took me into Parker's for an ice. He then left me to go and read the papers at the club on the front just opposite the octagonal house from which Millais painted his picture of the boyhood of Sir Walter Raleigh, who was born at Hayes Barton Farm near East Budleigh. My father commanded me not to eat another ice. Back home at lunch he asked me: 'Did you eat another ice after I'd gone?—'Yes, Daddy,' I said, 'I did. I couldn't resist it.' He was quite cross. I was a little confused; it would have been so easy to tell a lie. I felt I ought to have been rewarded for my honesty.

Her fox-trots were funereal but she was always game and would try anything however difficult, even *Dardanella*. As one became older and more sophisticated, so one would make more jokes about Mrs Parker's playing. Jack Semple, by the time he had reached the dinner-jacket stage, used to get rather restive and try to substitute his gramophone for Mrs Parker, but Mrs Semple was always very careful that the faithful pianist's feelings should not be hurt.

Mrs Semple's record introduction-gaffe at a children's party was told to me by my friend, Joyce Evans. (Joyce later committed the – in Mrs Semple's eyes – unforgivable sin of marrying a doctor who was a junior partner in the opposition practice headed by Doctor Vincent-Smith.*) Mrs Semple was introducing a very tall, rather awkward girl to a dancing partner. 'This,' she said, 'is Edie . . . eugh . . . eugh . . . eugh. Edie dances like a brick.'

Whenever a new family with children arrived in Budleigh Salterton the children would be invited to one of Mrs Semple's parties. If, when any member of the family was ill, they called in any other doctor than Semple, the children were never invited again. This system was one of the most ingenious for attracting patients that I've ever come across. I only wish it was still practised today. The Vincent-Smiths ought really to have countered with some opposition entertainments of their own, making use of Mark's Café opposite the Post Office, the rival establishment to Parker's. I dare say Mrs Vincent-Smith, a tall,

---

* I can't refrain from telling one story about this man. He was fitting a ring for supporting purposes into the uterus of a fisherman's wife, one of his patients. As he produced the ring he remarked gaily: 'With this ring I thee wed.' The fisherman's wife was not at all amused and there were no more free crabs for Doctor Vincent-Smith. I was particularly grateful to him because, when my passion for psychiatry was at its height, he took me, in 1932, over Exminster Mental Hospital, then a terribly depressing place. He didn't attempt to make any secret of the fact that one of his entertainments on his periodical duty visits was listening to the 'bad language' uttered by some of the lady patients. On the afternoon I went with him he got, quite literally, a sock in the eye, flung by a manic cook from one of the Budleigh Salterton hotels whom he had recently had to certify.

ultra-refined lady who, I believe, played the cello, thought that sort of thing beneath her. She was a very severe lady and once reproved Joyce Evans for laughing too loudly at the tennis club. 'My dear,' she said, 'you must never ever forget the Practice. A doctor's wife, remember, is always a doctor's wife.' Joyce told me she just managed to stop herself saying: 'Even in bed, I suppose'.

I made two new friends during that summer. One was an American boy, Travvy (Travers) Parkinson. His parents were elderly and came from Florida; they went back there after a few months in Budleigh Salterton. Travvy was good-natured and slightly scatty. Like all my holiday friends, he was somewhat older than me. I think he was just about to go to a public school. We used to go on bicycle rides together. If he ever fell off or had a puncture he would let loose a litany of curses which went: 'Damn, Curse, Hell, Blast, Shit, Bugger, Fuck!' This slightly shocked me but much amused my sister, Pat.

One of our common interests was thriller-reading. This had become quite a passion of mine. My parents had moved now to a house called Fernie Knowe at the top of Surgery Hill. My father bought it on a long lease for £1,300 from a methodist clergyman whose daughter had been running it as a boarding house. It was a solidly built mid-Victorian villa with big plate-glass windows. It had about an acre of garden and a beautiful position looking over the sea. My father, who always liked to make the best of anything he possessed, would point with his favourite stick, a light knobkerry, at the sea and tell us: 'You couldn't get a better view anywhere on the Riviera.' On a fine summer or even a soft bright blue December morning, he was almost right.

In a sycamore tree beside the tool-shed, overlooking Coast-guard Road, I built for myself a platform of boxes. I would climb up there and take my thrillers with me. I read Philips Oppenheim and William Le Queux and also detective stories from the Miss Warrens' lending library. The Miss Warrens were rather prim ladies; they were so shocked by Michael Arlen's *The Green Hat* that they kept it under their counter and only let it out to ladies whom they felt sure could not be corrupted. God alone knows what their reaction would have been to *Lady Chatterley's Lover.*

My father had a maddening habit of taking my detective stories away from me at night and reading them himself in bed. He read very fast and next morning at breakfast would insist on telling me who had done it.

'You realize, of course, that it's not the hunch-back dwarf or the butler. Those are just red-herrings. It's the spinster aunt all the time.'

'Oh, Daddy, do shut up. Now you spoiled it for me.'

'Beware, beware,' said Goethe in a remark that Freud was fond of quoting, 'beware of what you wish for in youth, for in middle-age it will most probably come true though sometimes in a manner which you least expect and may not altogether like.' If anybody had told me then that I would one day be paid – not much, never enough, but always something – for reading detective stories, I would have thought it a dream too good to come true. Now, when I sometimes have to call myself by an alarm clock at 5 a.m. in order to read a batch of detective stories and thrillers so that I can review them conscientiously, I realize the truth of Goethe's remark. About this time too, I developed a habit which has stayed with me, the habit of selling books. There was a second-hand shop in Budleigh Salterton then, run by an old Devonshire Jewess named Zillah Cowd. She had frizzy yellowish-white hair and darkened her eyes with kohl. She would buy anything and, at Travvy Parkinson's instigation, I would trot furtively down Surgery Hill with half a dozen books. What did I buy with the proceeds? Sweets, sometimes; cigarettes, for I was now a confirmed smoker during the holidays; and a gigantic hunting knife with a stag-horn handle. Now, when I sell review copies to my friends, the Clarke-Halls, in Wine Office Court, opposite the Cheshire Cheese – a practice which we literary hacks call running a cargo or taking a load to the knacker's yard – I remember old Zillah, though none of the Clarke-Hall family, least of all their wise and pretty assistant, Sally, look remotely like her.

My other new friend was Ronald D'Alessio. He remains to this day one of my closest friends and we now correspond regularly although there was a long period when we saw nothing of each other. Ronald is one of the strangest individuals I've ever met. In middle age he has turned mystical, almost saintly; in Somaliland, after the war, he organized at his own expense a clinic for sick African children. His head teems with schemes, including a major project for solving the problem of the world's food supply. Some of his ideas are wild in the extreme but he has good insight into himself and a highly developed sense of humour that keeps him sane. He is also an expert engineer. His father was a British Army chaplain. The family, originally Italian, had been settled in England for generations. Ronald's grandfather was a financial adviser to old Abdul Hamid, the last Sultan of Turkey. He had a fortune of over £100,000. He lent it all to a friend of his, a French banker who was in temporary difficulties and who embezzled the lot.

Ronald's mother and his two sisters, Violet and Carmen, lived in a house named Abottsham at the bottom of Fountain Hill, just above Station Road. The name Abottsham rings in my ears because Ronald was engaged in a little private war of his own with what he and we called the 'Oicks'. They would snarl at him out of the corners of their mouths 'Bottsham Swank'. He, very aptly for my face in those days often had a rather stiff, tight-lipped expression, they christened 'Tortoise Face'.

Ronald had a bad reputation which attracted me at once. He was considered precocious and morbid. He was said to stalk cats with a knife. His conversation was fancifully obscene. He told me a weird fantasy about a boy who had injected some of his spermatozoa into his pet mouse so that she produced a litter of creatures with tiny human heads and little human hands. Ronald was at his prep school and often wore the cap with blue and red rings. He looked utterly un-English with his dark brown eyes and olive skin, and must be a throwback to some of his Italian ancestors. He was a volatile and very emphatic talker. At first I was rather frightened of him, but I soon found we had common interests. He knew a lot about reptiles and lent me two books. One *Reptiles of the World* by Raymond L. Ditmars of the New York Zoo. The other was Dr Calmette's *Venomous Reptiles, Venoms, and Anti-Venine-Serum Therapeutics.* He also lent me Guy Boothby's *Dr Nikola* and its predecessor, *A Bid For Fortune*, in which Dr Nikola and his black cat, Apollyon, make their first appearance. Ronald, I can see now (and as he admits) identified closely with Nikola, the omniscient paranoid polymath, working out his elaborate plan of vengeance against the relation who had maltreated him as a child. Another of his favourite characters was Dr Fu Man Chu; he had, and so did I, a distinct tendresse for the doctor's beautiful Arabian ward, Karamaneh.

There was in Budleigh Salterton a schoolmaster-crammer, Mr Martineau, who gave boys coaching during the holidays and looked after boys whose parents were abroad. I went there to do some extra maths. There were only two resident Martineauites, Willy and Frank Buckingham, both of Mexican extraction. They and Ronald were at the same prep school and used to tell me horrifying stories about two bullies named Egg and Pike who caught an unfortunate boy and held his head in the lavatory pan. Mowden seemed almost a haven compared to this school. They quite alarmed me by talking freely about masturbation. Ronald and Travvy Parkinson had dug an enormous hole in the garden of Abottsham, and Ronald told me, with the peculiar sardonic relish which he then turned on people he thought stupid, how he had found one of their contemporaries sitting in the hole masturbating. I was one part amused and three parts horrified.

Ronald had a grandfather, a retired Indian civil servant, a judge, who lived with his sister, Ronald's great-aunt Amy, in a house called Nattore. Lots of houses in Budleigh Salterton had Indian names; Jubblepore, Rawalpindi, Cawnpore. . . . Ronald was none too fond of either his great-uncle George Manisty, or his great-aunt Amy. He used to give me excruciatingly funny imitations of poor old Amy, who suffered from chronic constipation, giving herself a suppository. I could imagine Ronald crouching down with his wicked little car to the key-hole of the WC door.

The evolution of Ronald from the prep school boy to the naval cadet was imperceptible apart from his change of clothes. He and I became two of the keenest connoisseurs of Turkish cigarettes in the west of England. Our cases were always crammed with several brands: Phillip Morris's Oxford Ovals, and the even bigger Blues were our favourites. Once I scored by discovering in a shop in Exmouth, Griffith's, an imported brand called Ottoman Empire. They were packed in beautiful tins with brownish gold lettering and blue paper, big fat oval cigarettes that burned with an occasional faint splutter as a fragment of salpetre ignited. They smoked beautifully cool and were the finest cigarettes I have ever come across. Ronald was also a pipe-smoker and beside his bed he had an elaborate Dunhill catalogue entitled *The Book of Smoke*. For cheaper smoking there were the B. Morris Russians and the B. Morris Turkish with a bright picture on the packet of a harem scene with plump odalisques reclining by a fountain, also Major Drapkin's Russians with a picture of the Kremlin on the packet.

My relations with my mother were rather good at this time. One evening she took me into Exmouth to see a film about Turkish atrocities in Armenia. It was part of some branch of the war effort. Ladies in Armenian national costume sold programmes. A lady at the piano sang 'Land of Hope and Glory'. The film was a propaganda affair but there wasn't much need to exaggerate Turkish atrocities. It was rather good, with some terrible whipping scenes when the young Armenian heroine was in the hands of a wicked Turkish commandant. The screen went all blurred at the critical moment. My mother was rather alarmed, thinking that it might be too strong meat for me. We walked home, passing through the pine woods that line the road and the railway at the top of Knowle Hill. There was one wood here which my sister had told me was called Suicide Wood because two ladies had gone in there and taken poison. My mother told me afterwards that on this walk I declared solemnly: 'Mummy, after this no Turk can expect mercy at my hands.'

My sister Pat was in some trouble these holidays. She had been expelled from Sherborne for the ridiculous offence of signalling to a boy with a window-blind. My parents didn't make much fuss. My mother went to see Miss Mulliner, the headmistress, who I imagine was a battle-axe type. Her parting words were: 'Mrs Richardson, I advise you to get that girl married off as soon as possible.' Pat wasn't unduly cast down; she went next to a Domestic Economy College at Gloucester, and afterwards to a school at Folkestone. She was a cheerful girl, a good mixer with plenty of friends of both sexes and all classes. Her passion was riding. My own relations with her were very variable. There had been a good deal of jealousy between us as small children and sometimes it would come out in bursts of senseless aggression and streams of insults. She felt, and I think with justice, that my mother spoiled me at her expense. I was jealous of her on the grounds that, being older and therefore more vigorous, she was closer to my father than I was.

About this time, too, was the children's play. I was roped in most unwillingly to play the lead, the Jack in the Box in the toyshop. Enid Baddeley, sister of Clinton Baddeley, a Budleigh Saltertonian of long standing and a cousin of Ronald D'Alessio, was Daddy Tackhammer, the proprietor of the toyshop. (The Baddeleys lived in Station Road; they had an immensely aged mother, Connie, a well-known figure who lived, partly as a

result of Clinton's devoted care of her, to be a hundred and six.
She was pleasingly eccentric and once arrived at a wedding
with her present unwrapped in her hand; it was a wastepaper
basket with a lot of dead wasps inside.)

There were two girl-star parts. One was the Fairy Bright
Eyes, played by Audrey Hutchinson, a slight, delicate little girl
with sugar-brown hair. The other was the French Doll played by
Creena Beattie, her cousin. Creena and I had to sing a duet:
'When a good good girl like me meets a bad bad boy like
you. . . .' This was sheer agony for me. I practised it with a
temporary governess, Miss White, whom my mother had
engaged for those holidays. We got through it all right and
Creena's business with her parasol was sensational. She, I think,
was rather taken with me, but I had already lost my heart to the
Fairy Bright Eyes. This was the first of my three appearances on
the stage of the Masonic Hall at Budleigh Salterton. In the
others I appeared in a grown-up cast as the page boy in Ger-
trude Jennings' *The Bathroom Door* in which Mildred Fulton
played the Prima Donna and Clinton Baddeley the young man,
and also as a boy of some sort in *Five Birds In A Cage*, about
people trapped in a lift.

8

Now we are back at Mowden again for the winter term of 1917. This was a stormy term. I suffered acute Ape-persecution and was often miserable. My work was poor. I retreated whenever possible into the library and read. I had one of my trash-reading fits on and read bound volumes of *The Scout* and *Chums*, also the adventures of *Jack, Sam and Pete*, two white boys and a Negro. In *Chums* there was a wonderful serial about a New World Hercules named Strong Man Saxon who wrestled with a gigantic Wild Western thug the size of a mountain bear. I was very much taken with the description of Strong Man Saxon's physique, with his hairless body and whipcord muscles, the Carpentier type. I also read a boy's book called *The Lost Squire of Inglewood*, a strange Oedipean fantasy which I've never forgotten. The setting was Nottinghamshire. The hero's father was an MFH. He had been swallowed up by the River Trent. Both his son and his wife refused to believe he was dead. In fact, he had fetched up in a huge subterranean cave where he had been tended by a black cat who would creep through a crack in the rock and bring him tit-bits. When he recovered he kept alive by catching fish. His son, when taken over Nottingham Castle by a guide, wandered off on his own and found a secret passage which led to the underground cave. The end came with an elaborately staged reunion. There was also, for good measure, a mild and only incipient love affair between the schoolboy hero and a schoolgirl named Griz.

There was another strange quasi-boy's book that fascinated me. It was about a clash between two boys at a public school: one rather coarse, the other, the hero figure, younger and more delicate but also athletic. They fought. There was an episode when one rescued the other from drowning. Later, in London, after they had left school, the hero, who had by this time become an expert boxer and fencer, finally thrashed the bully. That's all I can remember, but the atmosphere of the book was very strange, and the bully was a particularly sinister figure.

My reading was perhaps more miscellaneous during this prep school period than at any other time, though it has always been disorderly. Yesterday I started re-reading *Under The Volcano*, looked at a book on the origins of the French language, and finally read myself to sleep with P. G. Wodehouse. Forty-seven years ago I was oscillating between *The Cloister and the Hearth* which had been strongly recommended by BAS, a book on the internal combustion engine and *Tarzan of the Apes*. The most fanatical Tarzan enthusiast was Longden, who changed his name to Longden-Knott, as Knott was his stepfather. He was an architect and built the new Westminster County Hall; a dashing-looking person with slightly long hair. I much admired him at half-term. Longden raved about Tarzan and his apes, especially Akut who was Tarzan's PA. I shared his passion.

In spite of my habit of selling books, I did sometimes buy them. There was a second-hand bookshop in Budleigh Salterton opposite old Zillah Cowd's. It was kept by a dear old man named Ellis, gentle and bearded. He sold me for a few shillings a seventeenth-century treatise on medicine with prescriptions for the Queen of Hungary's Water and recipes for viper soup. Its age fascinated me. There my half-sister Mary bought a limp green sueded edition of FitzGerald's translation of the Rubaiyat of Omar Khayam. This captivated me at once. Mary, always kind, gave me the book and told me to cross out her name and write my own in it. I read the poem over and over again and soon knew it by heart. It exactly suited my thirteen-year-old mood. I'm all in favour of letting children read exactly what they like; they must form their own literary tastes. The trouble is that conventional educators incline to recommend the wrong

writers because of their ingrowing fear of decadence and cor-
ruption. Cyril Connolly has dealt with this very sensibly and
eloquently in *Enemies of Promise*. It is important that the young
should be encouraged to read good poetry as opposed to the
second and third-rate poetry that is often given them for prep.
Nonsense, of course, they love and will generally ferret out for
themselves.

I remember two lines of nonsensical poetry that I read at
Mowden:

> *Pretty Patty Honeywood I should like to jump*
> *Into your affections with a resounding plump. . . .*

Those come from *Verdant Green*, that early Victorian joke book
about a simpleton at Oxford. I loved Verdant Green and his
passion for Patty Honeywood; but my favourite character was
Mr Bouncer, the sporting undergraduate who kept a bulldog.

There was something about the atmosphere of early Victorian antic capers in which any hint of sensuality was strongly
censored that seemed very close to the Edwardian prep school
world: one felt that one was grown-up but somehow in a safe
way, without having to deal with the atrocious adult sexual
urges. Genuine nonsense poetry, the semi-surrealism of Lear
and Lewis Carroll, faintly terrified me. It was as if I feared that
my mind, or, if you like, identity, might disintegrate under the
spell of its schizoid, crazy logic. I tried to share Ovens's enthu-
siasm for the *The Hunting of the Snark* but couldn't go very far
with him.

Every Sunday evening after tea Mrs Snell would read to us.
One term she read S. R. Crockett's *Sir Toady Lion*. Crockett
was a novelist of the Scottish Kaiward school who also wrote
children's stories. One of these was perhaps the most senti-
mental book in the English language. It was *Sweetheart Travel-
lers*, about a father going on a bicycle tour with his little
daughter. I had read *Sir Toady Lion* and its sequel, *Sir Toady*

Crusoe, much earlier. It was one of my favourite books, all about the adventures of a family who lived in the Northumbrian country. The leading spirit was Hugh John Pickton-Smith. He led a miscellaneous band to recapture from the 'Smoutchies' – the local oicks – a ruined castle on his father's land which they had taken over. Hugh John's girl-friend was Cissie Carter, daughter of his father's friend, Colonel Carter. There was a tremendous erotic scene when Cissie had committed some act of negligence and Hugh John was about to hit her. There was a lovely drawing of Cissie wearing a kilt and tam o'shanter, standing with her back to the wall saying 'Hit hard, brave soldier!' The scene ended in a kiss. Sir Toady Lion was Hugh John's younger brother, a character of infinite resource who used to exploit his cherubic charm with revolting calculation. In the sequel he acquired a girl-friend of his own, a cousin named Saucy, who obeyed his slightest wish. These Crockett books were redolent of Edwardia.

Ma Snell also read us Sommerville and Martin Ross's *The Experiences of An Irish R.M.* which I knew by heart. I used to sneer rather haughtily to myself at some of her mispronunciations of Irish names. Curious how however hard grown-ups at this period tried to find 'suitable' books to read to children, they yet didn't seem able to avoid stumbling on erotic motifs. Barrie's *The Little Minister* was another that Mrs Snell read to us; I found it almost as titillating as *She*.

That term I got my first hand-strapping. The Ape had given me two stripes in succession. When I showed up the dreaded blue cheque to BAS at breakfast he grunted: 'Come to my study.' When I arrived he took out his ESA punishment strap from a drawer in his desk and seized my left wrist. It was exceedingly painful. When he'd finished beating my left hand he exclaimed 'Six!' When he'd finished with my right hand, he again exclaimed 'Six!' although he'd actually given me seven. My hands felt the size of boxing-gloves and smarted at contact with the cold brass knob of the study door.

Soon after I arrived home for the holidays my father got a letter from the Ape telling him that my general misconduct and lack of attention was a great worry to him and his brother, the headmaster. My father showed it to me and it made me feel nervous and depressed, especially as it ended with what sounded like one of those veiled threats of expulsion. My father grunted at me and seemed rather embarrassed. I couldn't for the life of me conceive what I had done that was so awful. My sister Pat, when we were alone, tried – cheerfully, for she was generally in more acute trouble at her school – to cross-examine me. She kept saying: 'But you must have done something more than that, surely.' I couldn't satisfy her curiosity and stuck to it that I was just a victim of Ape-persecution.

Perhaps as a reaction against this Ape-persecution, I bought at old Zillah Cowd's a large heavy-bladed hunting knife with a stag-horn handle. My previous knives, which had given me a good deal of pleasure, were of that Swedish variety in which the blade retreats into a beautiful wooden barrel; I had one of the biggest size that the local ironmonger stocked, but it never satisfied me because the spring clip, which kept the blade in place when it was out, was so weak that when I stabbed a tree it collapsed. I felt the new knife was a real weapon. One morning we went out for a walk, my sister and I and a young man of about eighteen whom she had collected, together with his younger brother and sister. We found a swan sitting on her nest. There was a tall sapling with a lot of branches growing close by. If, said the young man, we could cut down that tree, we could push her off her nest and get an egg. I whipped out my knife. He took it, looking at me with that indulgent amusement which his type adopts towards maniacs of all ages. We cut down the sapling and he and my sister pushed the swan off her nest. She stood up resisting, hissing fiercely, with her wings outspread, but was forced backwards. I rushed to the nest, going up to my waist into the marsh, and grabbed a large pale green egg, one of three. I arrived home in triumph with it and not a qualm of guilt about any suffering caused to the swan. I blew the egg into a bowl and insisted on the cook making it into an omelette for me. I ate it for breakfast the next morning and it tasted absolutely delicious without a trace of fishiness. By the evening I had quite a high temperature and spent the next three days in bed with what was called a chill. I loved being ill as a child, and some of my happiest moments were spent in bed – not very often, though, as I was by nature exceedingly healthy. Part of the pleasure came from being nursed by my mother, but I was equally delighted if ever I was ill at school. The sensation of a rigor or shivering fit coming on was a delicious thrill. This regressive tendency, for I suppose it was that, has remained with me, even though illness when one is grown-up can be marred by anxiety about earning one's living. To the saloon bar question: 'What would you do if you won the pools?' my answer is always: 'Go to bed for three weeks.'

During the next Easter holidays, which began early, the last big German putsch had started. On a cold late March evening I said to my mother: 'The war seems to be going very badly.' She said, 'Yes it is at the moment, but I'm sure God won't let the Germans win.' I was a little reassured. Did I feel terror of the Germans? I'm not sure. There was a blue book of German atrocities in Belgium, which included an account of mutilating women's breasts, that horrified and at the same time fascinated me. There was also a stock home-front German paterfamilias who used to appear regularly in jokes in *Punch*. My sister and I claimed my father looked exactly like him.

9

Nothing to report about the next summer term; but during the next summer holidays Budleigh Salterton was particularly gay. The war was now going well, in spite of the Bolshevik coup and the retirement of Russia from the fighting. My father had acquired a paperback entitled *Rasputin, the Rascally Monk* which I'd read eagerly; but the Bolsheviks did not impinge on me until much later. Several new families arrived. There were the Ashbys, father and mother, Iris, a very glamorous girl of nineteen, her brother, Tim, in his last year at Harrow, his younger brother Rupert and sister Margot. Pat chummed up with them.

Mrs Ashby must have been a woman of some character; a competent materfamilias with a touch of the old soldier about her. She and a lady named Mrs Shuckburgh, with one of the most dramatically large bosoms I've ever seen, founded a society called 'The Shrimps' who went about in a gang. Pat was an enthusiastic Shrimp. I purposelessly abstained; they were too hearty for me.

My new friend was Dick Girouard. He arrived in Budleigh Salterton with his grandmother, Lady Solomon, a marvellously *mondaine* dame. She used to drawl and called me 'Lard' and my sister 'Paat'. She was a splendid sight at church parade on the Front on Sunday mornings. Dick was just about to go to Winchester. He looked exactly as he does today with a sensitive slightly, tadpole type of face, and glasses. He alarmed me by telling me stories of fashionable house parties where the butler, when you arrived, gave you a plan of the house on which everybody's bedroom was charted. I was horrified. I once suggested to him that we should dig a cave in a field on the cliffs above the

Rosemullion Hotel and turn it into a night club. He looked at me and said: 'I think you're mad.'

He had some favourite jingles of his own which he used to recite: 'Oh for a weedy beard, a beard that is weedy and long', and 'Swan and Edgar be ye blest for the clothes in which I rest. Swan and Edgar be ye cursed for the clothes which nightly burst.'

His grandmother had taken a house in Station Road. One of our amusements was to make huge gunpowder bombs and set them off. They never really exploded but fizzed and roared with burst of flame, very satisfying fireworks. Dick had conceived a dislike of a girl named Margery Nash who lived in a house in Little Knowle. He insisted on chanting outside: 'Margery Nash fell down with a splash.' Opposite Fernie Knowe was an empty house. Dick and I crept into it and wrote on the walls with a burnt stick: 'The next occupant of this house will surely die of cancer.' We learnt afterwards from Pat, who was mildly entangled with the son of the owner of this house, that there was no end of fuss over this. Our inscription was discovered the next time a prospective buyer was taken over and started back in horror. I think the original idea was Dick's; his sense of the macabre was quite as strong as mine. Small boys periodically engage in outbursts of guerilla warfare against the grown-up world. One of my own activities which I used to carry out in summer was to sink the bathing raft by covertly pushing in the cork so that when the waves washed over it, it filled and sank. Gooding, the bathing man, knew that I had done this but could never prove it. It was a highly irrational piece of vandalist sabotage on my part because nobody got more pleasure from the raft than I did, and Gooding always retaliated by refusing to put it out to sea again for three days.

The peak of my memories of Dick at this period concern his aunts, Lady Solomon's sisters, a delightful pair of elderly ladies with interesting little idiosyncracies; one smoked her cigarettes through a silver ring like a miniature monocular lorgnette; the other affected mannish ties and collars, spats and a homburg hat. We used to play bridge with them. In their treatment of us small boys they combined kindness with sophistication. 'Dick, Dick, there's many a man tramping the streets of London because he forgot to lead out his trumps,' said the younger aunt. After the final post mortem we talked about ghost stories.

Both ladies were confirmed psychics and elaborately versed in the literature of the uncanny, including those late Victorian and Edwardian occult thrillers: *Dracula*, *The Beetle*, and Sax Rohmer's beautifully titled *The Brood of the Witch Queen*; they knew them all and gave us, in their husky, cigarette-addicts' croaks, detailed summaries of the most horrific features. I was delighted when they told me about the huge posters on the London underground advertising *Dr Nikola*.

At last: 'Perhaps, Dick,' the elder aunt suggested, 'you would like to walk part of the way home with your friend; a little outing will be an aperitif for you after all this smoke and cards.'

Overcoated and mufflered, we pattered out into the soft night. The air was dark blue, very still and milky with the light of a rising moon. Over the sea a mist hung low, and through it sounded, sharp and distinct like a cat's yawn, the drawling lap of the wavelets on the large bun-shaped pebbles. As we walked along the terrace we discussed with the utmost boldness M. R. James's *Ghost Stories of an Antiquary*, which Dick had lent me a few days before. We agreed that the most terrifying of them all was 'Oh, Whistle and I'll come to you, my Lad,' because, apart of course from the initial whistle, it might happen to any one: that awful face of crumpled linen . . . if an evil spirit took possession of one's bed clothes, as well it might. . . . We were overdoing it; the state of terror into which we had talked ourselves, though still partly counterfeit, was beginning to lay hold of us. By the time we reached the gate of my parents' house, Dick's teeth were chattering. He was too frightened to face the walk back and begged me to accompany him. I agreed, flattered by the appeal for spiritual protection from someone two years older than myself. But by now we had conjured up a really formidable host. The entire 'Brood of the Witch Queen' was at our backs. The mist over the sea was the old count himself, while his daughters, those delicious voluptuaries of the canine fang, were waiting behind the laurels. If we managed to escape all these perils and reach our respective homes unharmed, we should find our relatives had disappeared and the front door would be opened by a heavily bearded nun. Back at Dick's house the position was reversed. This time I was too frightened to walk home alone. Unless we were to tramp backwards and forwards till dawn, some sort of compromise had to be found. Finally we agreed that I should take the longer way round through the lighted main street: Dick should accompany me as far as the first lamp post, then gallantly return alone as one who

> *walks on*
> *And turns no more his head*
> *Because he knows a frightful fiend*
> *Doth close behind him tread.*

Altogether it had been a delightful evening, one of the most delightful that I remember during a particularly pleasant part of my childhood.

Dick also had two cousins, Valerie and Daphne, both grown-up. Valerie I particularly remember because she was a type that I much admired, tall and faintly masculine, with a contralto voice. She once wore, for no particular reason except that it suited her, a brown Peter Pan dress. I believe she is now married to a general. She entertained me by reciting a limerick:

> *There was an old man of Bulgaria*
> *Who would take his bath in the area.*
> *Said Jane to the cook*

'Oh, do come and look,
For I've never seen anything hairier.'

I have two more recollections of Dick, both from the summer holidays of 1918. My parents were away and I was left in the charge of my half-sister Mary. On my birthday, August 24th, Mary and Dick and I went for a picnic to Hayes Wood. One of our aims was to try to find an alleged stone altar – I am quite sure it never existed – which Dick's aunts had told us they'd heard was there and had once been used for druid sacrifices. It was a very hot close day and after a half-hearted search for the altar we drank cider for lunch and lay in the wood reading. I was reading *Quo Vadis?* and became dangerously inflamed by Poppæa's attempt to seduce the young Roman hero, nephew of Petronius. Another happy day. Not so happy was our expedition to Ottery St Mary. We bicycled, Dick on a magnificent green Sunbeam with a three-speed gear. We had tea at Colaton Raleigh and looked into the church and pretended to be frightened by a flapping noise in the tower. Somewhere between Colaton Raleigh and Ottery St Mary we quarrelled bitterly and parted company. I cannot begin to remember what we quarrelled about; nor can Dick who has at least as good a memory as mine.

There wasn't much reptile-catching during those holidays, but I did collect a splendid pair of common lizards, one, the male, quite green, the other, the female, light brown. I asked my father what I should call them and he said Oise and Scarpe, two rivers which were featuring in the news of the fighting in France. I was distinctly disappointed at such dull names.

During this summer Bob Goodwin at last succeeded in getting some sort of commission in the Army. Bob was a young man with a brown tooth-brush moustache and a very genial hearty manner. His father was a bottle-nosed retired major. Bob was a friend of Pat's and we all regarded him as an amiable joke. He used to spend a lot of his time sitting on a seat on the front wearing blue plus-fours. His conversation was limited. His favourite expression was: 'By Gum, a rocket!' He once assured me very solemnly that a certain café, the Blue Bird Café, somewhere near Piccadilly Circus was 'the wickedest place in town'. Years later, I tried to find the Blue Bird but it eluded me.

10

The winter term of 1918 began quite well. I was goalkeeper for the first eleven which was coached by Rex De Koven, a Cambridge soccer blue and former Old Mowdenian who lived in Brighton. I distinguished myself in a match against a rather posh prep school, Cottesmore, and was given my colours – a half-black half-red flannel shirt. The ceremony was always the same. Janet would poke her head round the dormitory door just as we were going to bed and say: 'Richardson, Mr A.P. wants you in the diningroom.' I trotted down in my dressing-gown and the Ape who was having dinner with Mrs Snell – BAS had always retreated to his study by this time – beamed and said 'Congratulations' and handed me the shirt. A few weeks later my colours were taken away from me. I was in an adventurous mood and had been caught running through forbidden parts of the house including the maids' dormitory, though I had not the faintest lecherous intention. This debacle coincided with Armistice Day. During break BAS suddenly emerged from his study carrying a rolled-up Union Jack under his arm, stalked down to the flag-pole by the shooting range, and ran it up. Janet came and called me in: 'Richardson, you can stop walking round. The Armistice has been signed.' We were given a half holiday and addressed by BAS who told us how much we and our country owed to Lloyd George. I don't think I got my beautiful black and red shirt back until near the end of the term. That night I dreamed that I was going to be hanged by Lloyd George on the weighing machine at Budleigh Salterton but somebody, I think my father, interceded for me.

De Koven, the soccer coach, was rather sympathetic to me during this difficult term and I developed a mild crush on him.

There was something faintly romantic, even dashing, about
him, beginning with his name. He lived in for part of that term
and had a minute sittingroom at the top of the house with a
battered desk and a large wicker armchair. I used to go up and
see him and he let me play his gramophone. My favourite
record was:

> Chong go back to Hong Kong. . . .
> Teachee peachee Melican song.

Once I found him looking very smart in a dinner-jacket and he
told me he was taking the evening off and going into Brighton
to dance at Sherry's. This appealed to the penchant for sophistication with which my sister had, unintentionally, infected me.
I don't suppose his night out was at all wild for he was a most
steady and respectable young man. Many years later I thought
about writing a short 'straight' thriller about a young assistant
prep school master who gradually gets drawn into and is
finally ruined by the Brighton underworld. Then I found that
Simenon had already written a novel on almost precisely this
theme, Le Disintegration de JPG. De Koven's character never
disintegrated but he died tragically young from some bone
disease. I remember him with affection for the relief he gave
me from Ape-persecution. It was remarkable what a difference
it made to find one grown-up who would treat one, if only
for a few minutes a week, on terms of equality.

Nothing to report about those Christmas holidays, except
one war-time echo from the Exeter Pantomime. The comedian
sang a song about army-dodging: 'You can call up my mother,
my sister and my brother, but for God's sake don't call me.'
My mother was delighted by this. Then I got flu and she gave
me to read Dumas's The Three Musketeers which turned illness into an extra ecstasy.

The next spring term the Spanish influenza epidemic went
through the school. The Snells, I will ever admit, were ex-
tremely conscientious about our health. Janet, who I don't

think had ever had a day's illness in her life, was tireless. So was Edith, the red-haired assistant matron who looked after our clothes. Edith was also guardian of the bottles of fountain pen ink. For a fountain pen fetichist like myself this filling of pens was an important ritual. I owned a bottle of ink with a rubber top which would fill any pen by a pumping action. Apart from that delicious rigor I remember little of flu itself, which killed almost more people throughout Europe than the war. Convalescence was spartan but I suppose sensible. We were taken off all work and told to sit about in sheltered seats in our overcoats in the March sun. I borrowed the Every-man edition of Shakespeare's comedies from BAS and read them all one after the other, falling in love with various heroines; but in *As You Like It* my favourite was not Rosalind but her cousin Celia, I decided that if ever I had a daughter I would call her Celia, a resolution I have kept.

Meanwhile, a term or two back, two new boys, rather older than the average new boy, had arrived at Mowden, the brothers Butterworth, both freckled, Jack with reddish curls and Reggie with dark curls. They were vigorous, rather sophisticated boys, with rich parents who had made money in Java. At half-term their father smelt of cigars, their mother wore dashingly short skirts, and their sister, Joy, pranced about on the terrace in a picture hat and carried a handbag. I heard Ma Snell whisper to someone: 'What a little minx.' Both Butterworths were good cricketers, especially Jack who was a very stylish batsman and delighted the Ape. I quite liked them and became friendly with Reggie, the younger of the two. He was temperamental and a tiny bit snobbish but cheerful and could be funny. They both spoke with faint traces of accent, Dutch, perhaps.

Another boy who fascinated me was Cox, dark, curly haired, very good-looking, also a good cricketer. The Ape was mad about him. He organized a play about the Queen of Hearts, in which Cox played the star part. There was an absurd song about 'The hearty party's ready . . .' The Ape was positively drooling; in the jungle of his unconscious, hearts and tarts were inextricably mingled. I myself later wrote a play which the fifth form performed. Jack Butterworth and I were German spies and ended up by being shot in the Tower. When the play was over Cox rushed up to me and said: 'You were absolutely ghastly, stiff as a poker.' The only one of my lines I remember was said by a policeman: 'I know a basement where there's a nice fat cook.'

Cox was rich, I should think. Anyway he always had the most expensive toys, fountain pens, soft green morocco note-cases. Every Sunday after lunch, during the rest period, sweets were distributed by Mrs Snell. Then a feverish process of swapping would take place. Cox would hold up a fountain pen and say 'Quis?' Someone would shout 'Ego!' and offer him their sweets for it. He seemed to have an inexhaustible supply because the next Sunday he would still be in the market. The rate of profit must have been fantastic. Why did I never succeed in cashing in? It can't have been that I thought it unethical to take advantage of his greed because I'm not all that honest and never have been. Probably I was too slow and dreamy, deep in a book. One of my pleasures that summer was reading *The Count of Monte Cristo*, borrowed from BAS with whom I was now on fairly good terms. It was a single-volume edition in very small print. I think it took me nearly a fortnight to finish. I read every word and went on reading it in bed by the summer evening light in the dormitory until the black print began to dance like swarms of flies. The ingenuity of the plot fascinates me to this day. It is wonderfully calculated to appeal to the paranoid element in all romantics. The wronged Edmond Dantes, who becomes, as the result of the Abbé Feria's tuition in the Chateau d'If and his legacy of the Spada's treasure, omniscient and omnipotent, and then spares at least some of his enemies and betrayers, is a perfect figure to identify with. Because of his sufferings he earns his great fortune; or so one feels when reading about him. Burt read *Monte Cristo* soon after I did and we exchanged enthusiasms for the book. We both had a passion for the Abbé Feria, about whom we raved to BAS. He was sympathetic and mildly humorous about the extent of Feria's learning. That summer I played for the second eleven and towards the end of the term the Ape graciously admitted, at nets, that he had made a mistake and I ought to have been in the first eleven.

Budleigh Salterton became even gayer, with amateur theatricals at which Tim Ashby sang a song, *My Cushion Girl*, addressed to Sonny's Fraser's third sister Marjorie, commonly known as Ginger, who had a passion for him. The Shrimps were much in evidence. My sister Pat had made two great friends. One was Betty Mossop, a long-legged fifteen-year-old, who drawled. My mother caught her looking in her writing desk and she remarked with total sangfroid, 'I love looking through other people's drawers. I always do it.' The other was Angela Rainsford, the daughter of a clergyman's young widow. Angela was tall and fluffy with a round face and a good deal of wit. I had been given some rabbits by two sisters, the Miss Miles, and one day, after Pat and Angela had been fondling them, I yelled: 'You beasts, you've made them stink of powder. Damn you.'

I was befriended by Dick Palairet, aged about sixteen, a naval cadet at Dartmouth. We were hares on a bicycle paper chase and went climbing together at Sandy Bay. Dick found a little chimney climb which he went up easily, to my admiration. He was very quiet and reserved, obviously one of those good characters. It was a bicycling summer holidays. I remember buying bottles of cherry cider at a shop in Littleham and broaching them by banging the green glass ball stopper on the step of my bicycle.

In the more sophisticated grown-up world there was an invasion by a troupe of pierrots, the Pom Poms, who settled on a site on the front. The older generation was deeply sus-

LITTLE VICTIMS

picious, but the younger people used to flock there of an evening. This was the first and last experiment of its kind; I don't know whether it was a flop or whether the Budleigh Salterton Urban District Council refused to grant them a licence again. There was a comedian with longish black bobbed hair, a cross between a present-day beat and Billy Merson. He sang songs like 'List to me while I tell you of the Spaniard that blighted my life', and 'I'm Tony the Swiss Mountaineer'. His jokes weren't anywhere near blue by modern standards but he managed to get them across with that clown's leer which is part of the low comedian's art. I think he had some talent. One evening Freda Gossage, then about twenty-two, a girl I much admired, came up to me with a pair of red-hot poker flowers and asked me if I would present them for her to the comedian. I felt quite the stage door johnny.

Another extraordinary character who spent most of his nights in public was a man of about thirty-six named Bunch Aldersey. He was a drunk, I suppose. He gave a splendid rendering at the Masonic Hall of 'I'm Reckless Reggie of Regent Palace'. I would sometimes find him stretched out on a seat on the front quite late at night. 'Can't sleep, old boy,' he would say, exactly as if I were a contemporary. 'Can't get a bloody wink of sleep. That's my trouble. Suppose it's still that ruddy war.' I told my father this and he snorted: 'War be damned. I don't believe he was ever near the war.' There was a story that Bunch had been horsewhipped out of a house in West Terrace by an old lady who caught him making love to her spinster daughter. I liked Bunch. He and his brother Laddie are both dead. Laddie was even more extraordinary. He had a brown face and very white teeth and just missed looking like a matinée idol. He always wore knee breeches and a spotted bow tie. He rode on his bicycle to every meet of the East Devon Foxhounds. No otter hunt, badger dig, or rabbit worry for miles around did he ever miss. His conversation was elaborately sporting. He clipped his g's and

99

pronounced nine as naine and seven as severn. Ronald
D'Alessio used to do a fine imitation of him.

Otter hunting was a local sport. I went several times. My
mother insisted that it was cruel, which indeed it is. Of all
blood sports I now think it is the most barbarous. The otter
is chivvied out of his native river and up a leet or cut. He can't,
being an air breathing mammal, stay under water for long and
his presence is easily detected by 'the chain' of bubbles as the
air comes out of his lungs. The otter hunters with their long
poles stand across the river and bang on the stones if he tries
to go upstream or down. I like to think now that they had
particularly cruel faces under their ludicrous grey bowlers;
I don't suppose they were more cruel than anyone else, but
there you are. Anyone who has watched otters at play, the
most entrancing and intelligent animals, and can still hunt them
must have something wrong with him, I would have thought.

The greatest adder hunt of my life took place one afternoon
during those holidays of 1920. I and a boy named Tom
Bramwell set out for the common on the right of the first
hole, the one I've mentioned, and in the space of an hour and
a half we killed six adders: four males, fine fellows with grey
skins on which the black zig-zag pattern showed up beautifully, and two brown females. One of the males suddenly
darted out between my feet, and I got the impression that he
was attacking me; I don't suppose for a moment he was. Tom
and I each took three very dead adders home and skinned
them. I rolled up the skins when they were dry and kept them
in a drawer with my ties. This was the last great adder-bash
of my life. Not long after it I read W. H. Hudson on the beauty
of the adder's under-belly and decided to reform and appreciate the beauty of adders. Had I known what I know now
I would have watched this common carefully; it was just the
place where one might have seen the strange ritual wrestling
matches between male adders at the breeding season. Now,
as I've said, it's all built over. *Nous n'irons plus au bois, les*

serpents sont disparus. But not from the forest of Fontainebleau.
As I write this now, staying with my friends Desmond and
Mary Ryan at Recloses, I have just caught a fine colubrine
snake, an Aesculapian. I was taken snake-hunting by Desmond's
daughter, Juliette, who promised me a *couleuvre* of some sort.
And there he was curled up in a hole in a rock. I had plenty of
time to observe him and make sure he wasn't a viper; then I
took hold of him. He bit me three or four times on the back
of the hand, little tiny bites, almost caresses though each one
drew a drop of blood. Then he became quite docile. I took him
back to London in a linen bag and gave him to my friend
Mr Lanworn, the herpetologist at the reptile house. My eye
for a snake is still sharp, but when I was a boy it was excep-
tional. Once, riding on the carrier of Ronald D'Alessio's
motor-bike, I spotted an adder in a hedge. I told Ronald to
stop; we routed it out of the hedge with a stick, picked it up
carefully by the tail and carried it to open space in a wood.
There we made it strike at Ronald's blue silk handkerchief.
It struck many times and each time the two little spots of
venom were smaller until by the end they were invisible.
We were in a state of exhilaration and Ronald began imitating
Laddie Aldersey: 'Did the adder strike naine times or severn?'

About this time occurred the Nancy Cooper incident. Nancy
was dark, a tall pretty flapper and a friend of Pat's. She had a
long, long pigtail and a rather wide mouth. Her father was
supposed to have made some money out of boots. Her mother,
Edith Cooper, was as pretty as her daughter and had a handicap
of 6 at golf. Poor little thing, she eventually threw herself off
the cliff. Personally, if I'd been married to Charles Cooper
I'd have thrown him off the cliff. I played golf with him once,
years later, when I was at Oxford, and found him forbidding.
His only eccentricity was to devise a long hole of his own
about a mile long, which he played as a kind of bye or after-
thought. I don't think he spoke one word. One shouldn't ever
judge these silent officer types until one knows them well, but

when one is an undergraduate, full of adolescent paranoia, one is apt to think they are madly disapproving.

I remember once, at the time of a big coal strike, Edith Cooper dramatically asking me if I thought it possible for Englishmen to be so cruel as to leave their pit ponies down the mines without food? She'd been reading the *Daily Mail*, no doubt. Suddenly she kissed me. How fascinating it would be, I often think, if one could revisit one's past life in one's present guise, with one's present experience, and see if one could change people. I would make for Edith Cooper like a shot.

Nancy was much tougher, though I don't mean the word in the pejorative sense, than her mother. She had a great eye for men. She wrote to me once at Mowden and said: 'I'm told Tim Ashby will be here again this summer . . . What's he like? He sings divinely doesn't he?' I had a great eye for Nancy, but as she was several years older than me there was nothing I could do about it. Once, on the beach, she stumbled and her short check tweed skirt flew up. I put up my hands in mock horror. Nancy lobbed a stone at me. It caught me in the eye. My eye swelled up. I wandered off on my own; it was quite painful. My mother put Pond's Extract on it, and Nancy came up to enquire. I liked that girl. Her parents had quite a lot of money and she had a good time. She married, twice, to my knowledge. One husband – I can't remember the order – was French; the other was a Budleigh Saltertonian, a rich one, Scotsman named Colin Methven, very generous. He too is dead. He'd been badly wounded in the neck and came down to Budleigh to recuperate. He brought with him a faint air of the Riviera. He gave parties in a house near the tennis club and poured out Veuve Cliquot as generously as if it was lager. Almost the last time I saw Nancy was in the train from Waterloo. Rather to my surprise, she had become quite literary; she'd been reading, on the recommendation of Romney Summers, Ronald Firbank. She'd kept her looks, and if she's alive, which I'll bet she is, I'll bet she's kept them still.

II

Back at Mowden I was in the Sixth Form under BAS and more
or less safe from the clutches of the Ape. I sat at BAS's table at
meals and talked to him incessantly. I felt quite fond of him
and forgot his outbreaks of savage puritanism. There was,
however, one more traumatic incident that term. There was
an epidemic of some sort in Brighton and Hove so instead of
going to the children's service at St Peter's we would be taken
for an afternoon walk by Janet. That Sunday we'd had rabbit
pie for lunch. I was walking with Ovens. Suddenly I felt a
violent gripe. 'Please, Miss Snell,' I said, 'I want to go outside.'
(To go outside was our stock expression for going to the
lavatory.)

'All right,' said Janet. 'We'll walk on slowly and you can
catch us up. Ovens, you can stay and wait for him by the gate.'
I think she produced some toilet paper.

I dashed through the gate into a field and started feverishly
undoing my braces. It was too late. Before I could get my
trousers down and my shirt up my bowels erupted. I managed
as best I could and said to Janet, 'Please Miss Snell, I'm afraid
I've had an accident.' Janet was reasonably sympathetic and
asked if I could manage the rest of the walk; we were due to
turn back, anyway, I could change as soon as we got back.
At Mowden I was told to get a change of shirt and pants from
Edith and have a bath and then come down to tea.

At tea everybody started sniffing and saying: 'There's a
ghastly smell of shit in the air'. – 'It's you, Richardson,' said
Dalrymple.

'It can't be,' I said, 'I've had a bath and changed.'

'It bloody well is,' said Dalrymple.

In despair I passed my hand over my hair and felt something caked. What had happened was that in taking my shirt off, which was of the pullover variety – this was before coat shirts were invented – some of the shit had stuck to my hair. I burst into tears of deep humiliation. Mrs Snell toddled up and I tried to explain. She told me to go up and have another bath and wash my head and then go to bed. I felt almost ill with shock. I climbed into bed in my new dormitory, India, and read Rider Haggard's *Cleopatra*. There was a little verse that appealed to me:

> *Ptolemy the piper played*
> *Over dead and dying.*
> *Piped and played he well,*
> *Sure, that pipe of his was made*
> *From the dank reeds sighing,*
> *O'er the stream of death and hell.*

It seemed most apposite to my mood. Presently Reggie Butterworth came up and sat beside my bed. He told me Ma Snell had said, when I'd left the diningroom, that nobody was to make fun of me because it was bad luck on me and might have happened to anyone.

'But you know,' said Reggie, 'you're an extraordinary chap, all the same. It's just the sort of thing that would happen to you. Do you know how clumsy you are? You always move stiffly, like a box. Why is it, I wonder?'

He was quite right about the stiffness of my movements. This has left me with age, or what I like to think may be maturity. I suspect it was a deep-rooted symptom of some inner dichotomy. But there could be a hereditary element here. My half-brother, Archie, for instance, although of strong athletic physique, a good horseman and strong swimmer, had the same curious stiffness in his movements. I never saw him in action, as it were; and my own hypothesis is that this stiffness is in some way connected with an inhibitory factor that acts when the individual is engaged in so-called normal social activities but may be suspended when the time calls for violence. Violence there was between Reggie Butterworth and me during the boxing competition. This was expected to be won by Roller, a big, rather fat boy, very light on his feet. He and his rival, Vokins, were both day-boys. I loved boxing and had been taught by a painstaking sergeant at Belmont, the day school in Blackheath. At Mowden we had recently acquired a new drill sergeant named Camies, pronounced to rhyme with chemise. He was kind and sedulous, wore knee breeches and a sweater with a floppy collar. I wonder now if he was an old pouf; some drill sergeants are, and not necessarily any the worse for it.

The Vokins-Roller bout went to Vokins for style. Reggie Butterworth and I had a terrific first round with a flurry of punches all over the place. In the second round Reggie hit me slightly low, quite unintentionally. Silly old Camies stopped the fight and disqualified him. Reggie burst into tears. I said I knew he hadn't meant to do it, and anyway I didn't think he'd fouled at all. In the final I beat Vokins easily and had him groggy by the middle of the second round.

Years later, at Oxford, Reggie and I went to box for Oxford against Woolwich. We were both scandalously untrained. I, then just a middleweight, had to fight a tall dark gunner cadet. I was in a foolish romantic-tough mood at the time and when we came out for the last round, I being slightly ahead on points, I shot a left at him immediately after shaking hands. Some old general who was refereeing called out: 'Stop boxing. You must shake hands properly.' I felt a hot flush of embarrassment. My opponent got the fight on points. And who should I see in the ringside but Peggy Barr, sister of Pat Barr, a Budleigh girl with whom I was madly in love when I was fifteen, or so. She was married to a gunner officer.

Afterwards at dinner I reminded Reggie of the time he had

allegedly fouled me at Mowden. The Woolwich cadets were putting us up for the night. Reggie and I, with our Oxford habits, were far too sybaritic for the bleak dormitory that was offered us, so we took a train to London and set out on a round of night clubs. Reggie was entangled or in love with a girl who worked at a night club called the Bullfrog. (This struck a strong Budleigh Saltertonian chord in me because in, or around, the period of this book my sister had a gramophone record called *The Bullfrog Patrol*, which I think was on the other side of *Kitten on the Keys*, and used to give me a delicious sub-thrill.) We hung around the Bullfrog and eventually shared a double room in the Cavendish and went back to Oxford next morning.

This story must be completed because years later I met Reggie in the train at Waterloo, with the girl whom he had married; she had a pretty face like a peke. Reggie and she and her sister were going to stay at the Rosemullion for the week-end. Reggie and I played golf and he seemed moody and depressed. We travelled back to London in the same carriage and the sister, a funny little thing with short cropped hair, and I, had a long literary conversation, mostly about Dostoievsky. Reggie's wife joined in quite intelligently. Both of them mocked Reggie and said: 'He's never read anything. He's illiterate.' The sister was Joan Werner Laurie, who afterward edited the magazine *She* and died with her friend Nancy Spain on the way to the Grand National in a plane crash. As a tail-piece I should mention that Reggie and his brother Jack both went to Harrow – just the school for them. Reggie was expelled for climbing out of his house and going to a night club in London. See how the wheel comes full circle. Both Butterworths are dead now, like so many of the people in this book; BAS, the Ape, Ma Snell, Janet, my parents, my sister Pat, my half-sister Mary, the brothers Aldersey, and many more.

The greatest boxing occasion in the history of Mowden was

before my time. I was told about it by Tom Falkner. Bobby
Gooch's father, Sir Daniel Gooch, a sporting baronet of typical
Edwardian vintage – his wife eventually divided her time
between bridge and a mixture of brandy and ether – came
down for the day to visit his young hopeful. He did himself
well at the Albion, lunching and drinking champagne with
Harry Preston, and turned up at Mowden half-seas over. It
was a wet afternoon and there wasn't a football match to watch.
So Sir Daniel insisted on the Ape organizing a boxing competition in the gym on the spot for which he would provide
cash prizes. The Ape, always ready to toady to a rich parent,
obliged. According to Tom, Bobby Gooch, who couldn't box
the compass and never willingly hit a fly, was forced to put
on the gloves. Tom said the Ape had told his opponent to
let him have an easy time. Sir Daniel kept bawling: 'Belt him
Bobby, you little funk. Belt him.' How I wish I'd seen this.
I have a quite clear vision of Sir Daniel coming to play bridge
at Redgates; he was a dapper little fellow in a grey suit and
blue shirt and highly polished tan shoes.

Sergeant Camies kept us in touch with the world of boxing
outside. Our hero was Carpentier, whom the sergeant, like
half the population of the British Isles, pronounced Carpenteer.
I had a sneaking sympathy for Beckett, whose yellowish gypsy
skin appealed to me, but Carpentier's lightning knockout won
me over. My own heavyweight hero was and has ever been
Jack Johnson. How I wish I could have seen this great and much
maligned Negro fight. Nanny Skinner once told me that Jack
Johnson used to practise his punches on his wife. I was duly
horrified though I think, even then, that the manifest improba-
bility of the slander may have registered. My father, as he often
told me, was a natural heavyweight and the idea of him prac-
tising his punches on my mother was totally absurd. I've read
everything, which isn't very much, that I can lay hands on
about Jack Johnson, 'L'il Arthur', as he was nicknamed. The
only two people I've ever known who met him are or were

my friend Dave Smith the Chicago Kid, and the late John Davenport.

Davenport's account was not too clear. Dave thinks Johnson was the greatest fighter of this century. 'He was marvellous. He was fast and he could punch. He could hit a man when and where he wanted. He could drop him when he wanted. He would say: "You gonna last three rounds" and three rounds was all that man would last. He would say: "I gonna hit you in your nose" and he'd hit you in your nose. The referee would say to him: "Stop talking, Jack!" and Jack would say: "All right, I'm gonna knock him out now," and he'd knock him out. There's no other man around who can do that but Clay.' Dave thinks Johnson could, at his best, have beaten Tunney, Dempsey, and Joe Louis. I asked him what he thought about Jack Johnson's refusal to fight Sam Langford after their one fight which Johnson won without much difficulty. Dave said: 'The truth is just the opposite to what they tell you. Johnson refused to fight Langford because he knew if he did he'd ruin him. He wanted to keep his title and then Sam Langford could be the next champion of the world. Johnson was as decent a man as you'd ever meet in your life. Believe me he was a good man.'

John Davenport met Johnson when he was doing a turn at a fair at Atlantic City and gave me a short report of a conversation with him. Johnson was then past sixty. John asked him how long he thought he could go with Joe Louis, then and now. Johnson said, 'I guess I could just about stay a round.' This story, which I think true, got distorted by collectors and manufacturers of Davenportiana – Davenport could be more than a bit of a Munchausen – into a story of how Davenport said he'd sparred a round with Jack Johnson. In 1959 I sat next to Tunney at a lunch at the Savoy which David Astor gave for him. I asked him what he thought of Johnson, who was before his time. Tunney was rather contemptuous, and said: 'He was flatfooted.' But Tunney was not too sound on the colour question.

It had always been suggested that I should go into the Navy.
It was my father's idea originally, but I'd accepted it willingly
ever since I was a very small child. I had a book called *The
Wooden Walls of Old England*. Like many Edwardian children
I wore a sailor suit; my cap had HMS *Dreadnought* on it. I had
a bosun's pipe, and in summer a linen sailor suit and straw hat.
In the Easter of 1920 I went up for my interview for Osborne,
or rather Dartmouth as it would have been, because Osborne
was liquidated that year. I stayed with my uncle Woodhouse
who lived near the Crystal Palace. It was a delightful house
for a boy to stay in, with lots of assegais on the walls. My bed
had a fur kaross on it. For dinner we drank sparkling moselle,
exactly what a twelve-year-old would most appreciate. My
uncle smoked a meerschaum pipe. I was slightly shocked to
find a copy of *La Vie Parisienne* on the table in his smoking-
room. My father was staying there. After breakfast they talked
about the Bible and I vaguely remember my uncle had some
rather interesting comments to make about Joseph in the pit.
Then my father took me along to St James Park where the
interview was held. It was in some makeshift huts that were
housing the overflow from the Admiralty. I was interviewed
by an admiral, a schoolmaster, and some civil servants from the
Admiralty.

The only detail I remember was that the schoolmaster
asked me to point out some British possessions on a huge
blank map of the world. I pointed out some and he asked
for more. I said: 'Oh well, almost anything that's marked in
red.' The admiral liked this very much. Then I had an eyesight test, in another hut, and my father saw me off at Victoria

after giving me tea at the Army & Navy, always referred to in our family as 'the Stores'.

I was told I'd passed the interview but failed the eyesight test. One was allowed a second shot, so a fortnight later I went up to London again and my father met me at Victoria. He took me into the stores' optician's department and asked the manager, a nice little Scottish Jew, to look at my eyesight. The manager put me through a very elaborate test. I remember he said something about a spiral and I corrected him pompously: 'You mean those concentric circles.' He said: 'There's nothing wrong with his eyesight at all, Mr Richardson.' By this time I was seeing black spots. My father gave me oysters for lunch as the most digestible thing he could think of. Then we went across to St James Park for the second test. I failed again and cried a little when Janet broke the news to me back at Mowden.

I have a feeling that if my father hadn't taken me to the optician's department at the Stores, I would have passed that second eyesight test; in which case I would probably have passed the written examination, for BAS's teaching was quite efficient and I'd been doing extra maths for two summer holidays past; and so I would have become a naval cadet. How long would I have lasted?

I was discussing this the other day with an intelligent retired naval commander of about my own age, now managing director of a new company which cleans ships' bottoms in a way that saves their having to go into dry dock. He said: 'The Navy, contrary to most people's ideas, quite likes romantic rebels provided they can be got to toe the line when necessary.' I said: 'Yes, but it took me nearly half a century to learn to toe the civilian line. I think I should have been removed around the age of sixteen or seventeen.' Ronald D'Alessio is inclined to agree. His own naval career ended when he was a sub-lieutenant. He was an excellent engineer but in one ship he got upsides with his captain and packed it in. I sometimes think he regrets this. I do; the thought of Admiral D'Alessio, friend of Mountbatten, perhaps even a civilizing influence on the Duke of Edinburgh, is a fantasy I cherish. D'Alessio, what on earth am I to do with Charles? Do you think you could possibly . . . Well, I mean to say . . . Oh, I see, so you think that's it do you? H'm. Never thought of that. Well, look here, will you have a talk with him? I'll tell you what, you come and stay in the yacht at Cowes and then you can pick your own time . . .' And in the next birthday Honours we would read that Admiral D'Alessio had been made a life peer for Services to His Country of a confidential nature.

Why I, who have always been unpractical, and of a literary temperament, should have ever conceived the idea of becoming an engineer astonishes me. But there was a short period when I pored over books about engineering and traced diagrams of internal combustion engines. Mike Villiers, who went to Oundle the same term and into the same house as myself, was a natural engineer and sailor, the son of an admiral. I looked him up the other day and, instead of finding that Commander Villiers had retired, there he was: a Vice-Admiral and Governor of Guernsey. I shall make certain that he reads this book. We were close friends towards the end of my days at Mowden and I'm surprised he hasn't come into my mind before. He once sent the entire sixth form into hysterics by his rendering of the line,

Nobly, nobly, Cape St Vincent to the northwest died away . . .

pronouncing 'nobly' to rhyme with 'knobbly'. 'You ridiculous booby,' roared BAS.

My interest in science, I now think, was part of some sort of romantic wish for power. I'm surprised I didn't want to become a doctor. I did, in fact, specialize in zoology at Oundle and started to read zoology at Oxford. If a counsellor had whispered into my ear the word 'psychiatry' I think I might have had a paranoid vision of myself as the wise reader of human hearts, with a consulting-room in which beautiful American heiresses poured out their woes; or even Dr Richardson, Medical Superintendent of a huge Mental Hospital. Anyway, I wanted to go to Oundle because it specialized in science. Mike Villiers showed me a prospectus. My father liked the idea of the school and went with my mother to see the headmaster, Sanderson, H. G. Wells's friend; my mother got on particularly well with him; they cracked jokes together about the Sinn Feiners. My name was put down.

At Mowden science didn't exist. Every Thursday there was a long mid-morning period during which BAS took those boys who were learning Greek. We others attended Mr Pearl's lectures. Mr Pearl was a Brighton prep school institution. He was a short plump man who wore a black coat and striped trousers and a black tie with a pearly pin. He had a moustache and gold-rimmed spectacles, and was supposed to be a German. His lectures were elaborately illustrated by devices which he brought with him in a wooden case. One was a Whimshurst machine which delighted us by its blue sparks. A star turn was provided by the multicoloured Geisler tubes. Mr Pearl had beautifully neat upright handwriting, very small and clear, of the kind ascribed to scientists by the writers of crime fiction. I suppose I must have attended more than a hundred of his lectures but I cannot remember any details whatever. Later, during my last year or so, instead of going to Mr Pearl, Ovens, Sykes (a nice quiet strong-charactered boy) and I used to do extra maths with a Brighton maths coach named, I think, Field. He had a ragged brown moustache and smelt very strong indeed, a sort of cheesy smell; I daresay there was some drink mixed up with it. Ovens, on whom he had a slight crush, used to wrinkle his nose. Mr Field treated me with good-natured contempt. Once I got very enthusiastic about graphs and traced the curve of a spiral on squared paper. I think Mr Field was a good teacher. He used to make geometry interesting and draw figures freehand very quickly with a stub of pencil, but most of the time I would be dreaming. Why didn't he teach us the calculus? BAS was also a good teacher in his way, thorough and very painstaking. He could be funny. I remember him stumping about the form room using a rolled up map as a stick, in imitation of some classical worthy. And when doing Virgil he once remarked: 'Goddesses were great users of scent.' I liked that. My conversations with him at tea used to get more and more interesting – to me, anyway. Once I stumped him by remarking: 'Sir, every point in the universe must be the centre of a sphere of infinite radius, musn't it, sir?' I have since learnt that this, according to Einstein, is a popular fallacy, but I regarded it as a great discovery.

BAS lent me his own books. I read nearly all Scott and Dickens and Josephus' *History of the Jews*. I also borrowed his copy of Victor Hugo's *Les Misérables*, in which a batch of pages in the middle were clipped together. Naturally I unfastened them. The clipped batch contained the story of Cosette's mother, the poor little tart. I didn't read much poetry as a boy. We learned by heart Macaulay's poem about the Armada, and that rather tedious speech at the beginning of Henry V about the bees. We had a rep book, *Lyra Heroica*. When I came, in this book, to

> *Sound, sound the clarion, fill the fife,*
> *To all the sensual world proclaim;*
> *One crowded hour of glorious life*
> *Is worth an age without a name,*

so engrained was my puritanism that the world 'sensual' gave me a slight guilty frisson.

I had one brief religious phase. It lasted about ten days. I was given by Mrs Snell a short book of very Protestant prayers. I read it with devout concentration and prayed like smoke.

I prayed to be better at maths. No result. The religious phase ended abruptly.

The Snells had one son, Alfred, who was a Winchester scholar. He was short and plump and pink and kind. Once he came home early for the holidays and took the sixth, praising my Latin unseen very highly. Alfred had made an elaborate family tree of all the Gods and Godesses of Greek mythology and their inter-relationships. When I last saw him he was at New College, on the way to becoming a clergyman. It was during my first term and I was being sick into the snow.

As one grew older churchgoing at Mowden offered more concrete attractions than the whoredoms of Aholah and Aholibah. There were always the girls' schools. Once at Preston I had a delicious experience. In the pew in front of me was a pretty girl with brown hair. She was clutching a pink handkerchief that obviously contained something vital. Her neighbour was covertly giggling. During the lesson – incidentally, for any children who are still forcibly taken to church, let me recommend the lessons as the time to flirt or amuse oneself because they, especially the Old Testament, have a hypnotic, riveting quality; the sermon is a dangerous time which generally fails to hold the attention of the authorities who let their eyes wander and start doing detective work – during the lesson, she put her pink handkerchief on the pew shelf in front of her. I leaned forward and saw what was inside it: a live field mouse, brown as her hair. I fell in love with her instantly, but never saw her again.

At the children's services at St Peters, Hove, there were also girls' schools. There was one girl with dark hair and a fringe who fascinated me, but I never managed to sit anywhere near her. Tim Smallwood did, though. And during a missionary sermon which became famous he started passing her notes and she wrote a letter to him at Mowden. The missionary sermon was phenomenal. It was delivered by a

visiting clergyman with the most extraordinary whining
delivery I had ever heard. The missionary about whom he
was telling us was named Mr Porter and had a devoted wife.
The only thing Mr Porter seemed to have done was to walk,
whether it was through a desert or a jungle I don't remember,
but how that man walked. 'And Mr Porter and his wife walked
on,' the clergyman kept saying. I wish I could tell you just
how he said it. For the next two days we were all saying
nothing else.

Budleigh Salterton was quiet that winter. Abottsham, where
the D'Alessios had lived, was now occupied by a Mrs Calvert
and her daughter Vivian. The Calverts were Irish and my
mother discovered at the bridge table that they were cousins,
very remotely but indisputably so. Vivian was about nineteen,
fair, not unpretty, very jolly. She asked me and Pat to play
bridge. We called each other 'coz'. She mentioned that there
was a *thé dansant* at the Beacon Hotel in Exmouth the next
Saturday afternoon, and she thought it might be fun to go.
So I went with her. I wore my best suit from Pinder and Tuck-
well in Exeter; I'd been wearing long trousers for some time
now. We went by train to Exmouth. Vivian carried her
dancing shoes in a paper bag. She discovered that the heel of
one was frayed and the white wooden block showed through.
I produced one of my fountain pens and inked it over for her.
She was giggling all the five miles from Budleigh Salterton to
Exmouth and we remained in a state of euphoric giggles
throughout the *thé dansant*. The Beacon, at which I stayed
the other day when visiting my friend Alice McClintock
whom I met when I was sixteen, is now newly decorated
and very comfortable – that row of houses looking over
the mouth of the Exe is enchanting – but in 1920 it was
on the stuffy side. The diningroom was large and long with a
terrific marble mantelpiece and a huge coal fire. The proprietress, in black, had a cold and kept sniffing. Vivian became
quite hysterical and so did I. I can't remember much about the

jeunesse of Exmouth, whom I later came to know very well. One fact I do quite definitely recall: a hunchback dancing with a rather tall girl. Vivian and I, being superstitiously inclined, tried to get near him so we could brush against his poor little hump for luck. Another ecstatic afternoon. We giggled all the way back in the train. We never again achieved quite such a close rapport and fairly soon afterwards Vivian became engaged to a tall, dark Cambridge Rugger blue named Humphreys and married. I wonder, if she ever reads this, whether she will remember the *thé dansant* at the Beacon.

*   *   *

And now I must back-track a bit. I've left out some rather significant Mowdenian incidents. During the summer term, approaching my thirteenth birthday, I had become Captain of a dormitory, India. I was one of the least disciplinarian of captains. I encouraged talking after lights-out and Janet's goodnight; and a nice little redheaded boy named Kitcat – the names at prep schools always fascinate me: Miskin, Grogono, Littlehales, Dove, I would enjoy a roll call of all the odder names one has ever heard – used to get into my bed and creep down to the bottom and make a tent. Our relationship was entirely asexual – I hadn't as yet had one of those erections that mark the onset of puberty – but Janet caught us and I was reported to Mrs Snell and demoted from the captaincy of India. For a time I was made to sleep by myself in a room which was used for music. It was occupied during the daytime by 'Chipper' Evans, the girl who taught the new boys and gave music lessons to juniors. (A dark lady, Miss Hume, taught the more promising ones and occupied a room next door to Edith's clothes department. There was a metronome here and Burt and I used to go in and do table turning, our part of the great post World War One spiritualist wave.) I remember in 'Chipper' Evans' room a piece of music with a forest pool on the cover; I gazed at it before going to bed. How kind and tolerant Mrs Snell seemed over this, as compared with BAS's savage puritanism! She made me come down in my dressing-gown to her drawingroom and talked to me. 'You,' she said, 'are one of those boys who can do a lot, but it depends on whether God or the devil gets you.' She kissed me. Was I alarmed by the reference to the devil? I think not. As I said earlier on I was never frightened of the devil. When I read Lear, Edgar's line –

The Prince of Darkness is a gentleman,
Modo he's called and Mahu

instantly appealed to me. Once, when looking at television, slightly drunk, I saw Hitler in a newsreel, part of a rehash programme about the Nazis, and I had a fantasy that he was the devil himself. The only thing about this singularly revolting creature that in any way ever appealed to me was his sense of humour, which did indubitably exist: savage and doglike, a genuine cynic. I deny, now, that he was ever the devil, who, with all his faults, must once have been a gentleman in the literal and only true sense of the word.

The next term, to continue my dormitory history, I was allowed to sleep in a small attic dormitory with Mike Villiers and Burt. Mike was a keen reader of the Book of Revelation. He insisted that it was all true or would come true. 'And there shall be no more sea,' he intoned. 'Just you think what that means.' Coming from a future admiral, it was a significant remark. I wonder whether he ever looks out of Government House, Guernsey, in anxiety lest the sea has gone down the drain. He also drew my attention to some of the prophecies of Ezekiel, especially that flying machine. His father, Admiral Villiers, had invented a device for trapping torpedoes, I think it was called the paravane, about which there was a lot of dispute in naval circles. Meanwhile Trub (Burt) would entertain

us with songs from London shows which he and his sister
had been to. One was 'Madam, will you walk? Madam will
you walk and talk with me?' It went on: 'If you give me a
Rolls-Royce car and all the makes there bloody well are'
etc. . . . Dear Trub. But whatever possessed him to take all my
geometrical instruments, a beautiful Victorian set which I
didn't even know how to use, and stick them into the floor
of the Sixth Form room? I was furious and flew at him. Janet
knew that I had right on my side and let me 'lick', to use a
Mowdenian expression, Burt. Another thing he did quite
early on in my career was to do a turd in my chamber pot.
I got a stripe for this and complained bitterly and the stripe
was revoked. I remember the turd now; it had a distinct look
of Trub about it.

There was one boy of whom, at this time, I made a pet,
although relations with him were entirely sublimated. He
was a small boy in his second term whose dark hair and slightly
sticking out teeth gave him a faint look of a marmoset.
He was always in trouble, I never quite knew why, and spent
almost as much time walking round as Burt and I had done.
I once took him into the carpenter's shop, or more likely
found him there in tears, and put my arms round him and
hugged him and said: 'You must try to be good.' There
was another little boy whom I made a pet of for a time,
but that was a year or two before. He was a day-boy named
Osborne, very small with a scarlet face. He used to get teased
rather a lot and when teased he would put his hands to his
ears. Because of this I called him the Deaf Adder, which
he came rather to like. Being a day-boy, the Deaf Adder had
access to all sorts of things. He brought me in a mouse-trap,
which I set under the classroom floor and caught a sad young
house mouse whom I let go. He also brought me a fine length
of brass piping, beautifully straight, which made a splendid
blow pipe with, for ammunition, pellets of chewed up blotting
paper. And he found for me a fine beetle, Hercules, whom I

used to race over my desk. I wonder if the Deaf Adder's alive; I would like to salute him across the years.

My last summer holidays, when I was rising thirteen, was the Guy Butler summer. A lot of Old Harrovians had descended on Budleigh Salterton. There was a Collins or two, a poet named Archie Gordon, and Guy Butler a famous Cambridge quarter-miler. My contact with them was J. A. R. S. Stevenson, another Old Harrovian, who was one of my sister's young men. He is now, Lord save us, a Christian Science healer, having tried his hand at all sorts of things including wrought-iron work. Guy Butler was an enormous fellow with a big ugly face and a good deal of charm. I hero-worshipped him; he took an innocent fancy to me and drove me about in the sidecar of his motor-bicycle. Once he came to stay for a night and delighted my father by the enormous breakfast he ate. Later he organized a small camp on the far side of the Otter; he asked me to go but my father said, no, I could go for the day but was not to stay the night. Guy used to write to me from Cambridge and his letters gave me a certain amount of éclat at Mowden. Archie Gordon I saw rather more of. We travelled to London together with his mother who by way of being an amateur medium, as were a good many ladies in those days; the post-war spiritualist boom was well on. (Once a professional fortune-teller descended on Budleigh Salterton and lodged quite near us in Coastguard Road. At that time we had a house-parlourmaid nicknamed behind her back by my mother and me 'the Chimp'. The Chimp, soon after she'd arrived, went to consult the fortune-teller. She told my mother she had been warned: 'You'll be very unhappy in your new place.' My father, when he heard about this, grabbed his knobkerry, put on his homburg hat, and dashed down to the police station. 'We'll get that damned woman out of the place right away,' he said.)

Now we arrive at the 'sudden onset of puberty'. For me it arrived with my passion for Bradford. It came on me suddenly, with a rush, in the winter term of 1920 when I had just turned thirteen. Bradford was a charming boy with brown hair, a fine nose and a rather wide but thin mouth. He lived at 4 Upper Brighton Road, Surbiton. He was an inside right forward in the soccer team. I woke up one morning and found I adored him. Whenever I could I would sit next him and put an arm round him, and stroke his rather bony knees. Once we went to play St Ronan's at Worthing, a posh prep school run by a famous soccer player, Stanley Harris. In the taxi I sat next Bradford and hugged him. I never kissed him and never tried to touch his parts, but I was as much in love with him for a fortnight as I've ever been with anyone. Then, just as suddenly, I fell right out of love with him and he ceased to mean anything to me. I saw him later, at an OTC camp at Strensall in 1923, when I was at Oundle and he was at Rugby. We talked a little about Mowden and were rather shy of each other.

Assistant masters came and went. I was involved in one *cause célèbre* of which even now I feel faintly ashamed. Richard Lee and Sanderson had been making a lot of Christian Science propaganda, or so Chaplin, the Badger, and I thought, so we approached BAS and said we didn't think it was right that we should be subjected to this. BAS listened sympathetically. The next Sunday evening Ma BAS, after her reading, talked about the Christian Science propaganda and said how important it was that 'big boys' should report anything that was wrong. The Badger and I felt a righteous glow. (I wonder, by the way, what happened to him. He was a clever boy and had the most extraordinary handwriting I've ever seen. It looked like twisted barbed wire.) A day or two later, BAS sent for us and said he'd talked to Lee and Sanderson and they denied that they'd ever made any serious Christian Science propaganda and he thought we ought to apologize to them, so we went up to their little sittingroom and Sanderson said: 'Ah, when I heard those feet on the stairs, I said to myself, "That's Richardson and Chaplin" ' I forgot what we said, but

the atmosphere was friendly enough. I think the Badger and
I were a bit priggish. In my own case I had a throwback to my
father and his struggles with Prentice, his under-gardener, who
was a confirmed Christian Scientist and refused to have a
doctor to attend his son, Dick, with whom I used to play at
Redgates. Lee and Sanderson left not long after. They were
succeeded by a small, simian man called Mr Came, who was an
expert carpenter, and a tall rather smart person, Mr McMahon.
He had various literary prejudices. He told me that the prose of
Richard Blackmore in Lorna Doone was some of the finest in the
English language and turned naturally into blank verse. He had
a passionate hatred of Voltaire and described with loathing the
bust of Voltaire in the Comédie Française which he said was
like 'a grinning devil'. Strange aberration. Another great
admirer of Lorna Doone was Derek Wigram who went to
Winchester and afterwards became headmaster of a school in
Somerset, Monkton Coombe. He was a plump, compact little
boy with reddish hair and freckles. I had a faint crush on him
and he tried once to teach me Greek. He was good-natured and
kind. We often travelled home together because he lived near
Braunton in North Devon. Once in the train on the way to
London Bridge there was a child in the carriage who had some
kind of sore on her face which had been plastered with black
ointment. Whether it really smelt as bad as we made out I'm
not sure, but it was a private joke between us long afterwards.
'Black ointment,' we would whisper into each other's ears and
shudder.

It shows you how unpredictable small boys can be that Derek
should have once been guilty of an unexpected piece of mental
cruelty. I'd told him I'd just had a letter from my mother telling
me that Sandy, our beloved bulldog, was dead. A few minutes
later he said: 'I'm jolly glad your rotten old bulldog is dead.'
I was amazed. Later he came to me and said he was sorry he'd
said it. I had a little soapstone skull then and I went off alone
into the carpenter's shop and smashed it to fragments with a

hammer. Dear Sandy, he was one of the sweetest-natured dogs I've ever known. When he was about four my mother nursed him through double pneumonia, sitting up for two nights with him. For some time he'd been getting old; his teeth were bad. Bulldogs are very short-lived. During the winter holidays my half-brother Wilfred had been staying at Fernie Knowe. He wasn't in the sweetest of moods, having been a prisoner of war in Germany for four years and also having married a woman he didn't really want to marry; he had teased Sandy by blowing the bellows at him as he lay snoring, and made jokes about his breath. I was furious and rushed out of the drawing-room in tears. I could have killed him then.

That winter I made a new friend in Budleigh Salterton, Vera Chesney. She was a widow whose husband had been a colonel in an Indian cavalry regiment and had died fairly recently of cancer of the throat. Her son Kellow remains one of my closest friends. Vera was a most intelligent woman, daughter of an Indian civil servant named Moule, who had become a judge. She talked to me as if I was an equal. There was something distinctly Kiplingesque about her; she might have figured in *Plain Tales From The Hills*. She had two greyhounds, Tuan and Kelpie, and once shocked my mother slightly by yelling: 'Tuan, damn your bloody soul, will you sit down.' I used to take these two out to Short Wood and once they put up a rabbit and coursed after it and killed it, graciously allowing me to take it away from them. I was delighted, and so was my sister Pat, who liked to encourage any latent sporting proclivities. Vera's son Kellow, then called Robin, was about six at this time. I took him out lizard hunting but he was bored blue. Even at that age he was a fluent conversationalist, but sometimes he suffered from fits of temperament. We had him to look after for the day and Vivian Vaughan-Cox, a friend of Pat's and cousin of the Chesneys, did her best to keep him entertained by playing and singing some of Delysia's songs. There was one the lyric of which has a very strong 1920 period flavour:

Ninon was witty
Ninon was pretty,
Ninon was a naughty girl . . .

It went on about how she lost her ring and:

They found it in the red room
Which was really Louis' bedroom,
Ninon was a naughty girl.

Goodness only knows what six-year-old master Robin made of
this one.

13

About this time I began to have strong sexual stirrings. During the winter holidays I had smoked a BDV cigarette, and in the packets of these there were 'silks' instead of the usual cigarette cards. This had a most peculiar aphrodisiac effect on me: I had an erection and felt dizzy. During the Easter holidays of 1921, just before my last term, I was out lizard hunting. It was a hot blue spring morning, with the grasshoppers chirruping away like mad, and I suddenly found myself with an enormous erection, feeling almost as if I was in a classical landscape. It would have been the moment for a nymph to appear and instruct me. That evening after tea, alone in the drawingroom, I masturbated for the first time. I enjoyed the sensation but was immediately seized with a pang of guilt. 'You must never do this again,' I said to myself. However, I compared notes with a Budleigh Salterton chum a bit older than myself, and some, anyway, of the guilt was assuaged.

But trust old man BAS to stoke the puritan fires. That summer term, one evening in class, I was tentatively and rather absent-mindedly masturbating inside my trousers. BAS summoned me to his study.

'Do you know that was a very wicked thing you were doing in class today? How far had you got? Did you get an – er – pleasurable sensation?'

'No, sir,' I lied.

He gave me a book which was the official manual of sex instruction for prep schools. It was called *Healthy Boyhood*. It began with the birds and the bees and ended up with this sentence: 'And if, when you get to your public school, another boy ever tries to get into your bed, report him instantly to your housemaster.'

The routine with *Healthy Boyhood* was that on the last day of the term those who were leaving would be taken to a place apart by the shooting range, where BAS used to read us *Marmion*, and given a copy of this book. I, previously instructed, was spared this ordeal, but one tactless boy asked: 'Sir, sir please sir, why isn't Richardson reading it?'

'Because he's read it already,' growled BAS.

I did one thing that term which I remain ashamed of. I was captain of Australia and I slippered Mike Villiers, one of my best friends. I don't remember the pretext. Mike was furious and threatened vengeance when we both got to Oundle.

On the credit side, I was captain of the cricket eleven. The Ape was reluctant but nothing could be done. I was an unconventional batsman who tried to hook balls round to mid-on, and a good bowler though inclined to bowl too fast and lose my length – everything that most displeased the Ape. We started off in fine style by thrashing Marlborough House, but by the time we played Rottingdean our fielding and my moodiness had caused a collapse. Afterwards the Ape demoted me and made Rock captain instead.

This match was a real tragedy. Rottingdean, a neighbouring prep school, had a nice-looking, youngish headmaster named Parker, with a young and pretty wife. Their son was at Mowden. Rottingdean also contained a boy named Bonham-Carter who was six feet tall and strong in proportion. If you played against Rottingdean the only hope was to get Bonham-Carter out before he got set, otherwise he would make anything between seventy and a century. This match Bonham-Carter was in his best form. I bowled and bowled. Mr Parker, in plus fours, was umpiring at square leg. I bowled a long hop. Bonham-Carter pulled it round, the ball travelled a few feet above the ground and hit Mr Parker with a fearful crack on his shin as he sat dozing on his shooting-stick, thinking, perhaps, that it was rather a relief it was Bonham-Carter's last term. He fell off his shooting-stick and had to be carried off the field. The awful thing was that the wound went septic and he died of it a few weeks later. So between us Bonham-Carter and I could, I suppose, have been said to have boy-slaughtered, however inadvertently, a prep school headmaster.

The greatest excitement of this, my last term, was the adventure of Burt and Ovens. They took to creeping downstairs at around one o'clock in the morning, raiding the larder, smoking BAS's cigars and drinking his port. Once I went with them; but only once; my nerves wouldn't stand the strain. We sat in BAS's study and Burt took the ESA punishment strap from its drawer in BAS's desk and swished it through the air. Of course they got caught in the end. Burt, who had no shred of caution, went and sat himself down in Ma BAS's office and typewrote a letter to his sister, the former VAD – I should like to have met her – telling her exactly where he was and what doing: smoking a cigar and drinking a glass of port. He went and left this letter in a library book which Janet picked up and read, and that was that. A bottying for Burt; he didn't give a damn. Adorable Burt, how he brightened one's life. He is dead now, and so is his younger brother, Oliver, who was an actor of much promise. The last time I saw Burt major, was towards the end of the war in a restaurant in Percy Street, now kept by my friend George, from Cyprus who does a balancing act with glasses on his head that defies belief. Burt was in major's uniform that exactly matched his greenish complexion. We talked a little about Mowden and he told me had enjoyed himself there no end. I was too tactful to mention that I'd heard about the rest of his school career. He went to Haileybury and was expelled for breaking open the school safe. Then he went to Dover College. By this time he had outgrown his Raffles phase.

After the bottying we were told that They knew other boys had been doing the same thing, and if they owned up there would be no punishment. So Ovens and I and Mike Villiers went and confessed that we'd each gone downstairs once.

I passed my common entrance fairly satisfactorily. The last day came with the *Healthy Boyhood* reading, as I've told. After tea I had a sudden access of remorse or nostalgia, I don't even now know what to call it. Everyone else had left the dining-room; BAS was still munching away. His habit of eating a large high tea with us, while we ate school food, was something we always resented. Madly we envied him; scotch egg was one of his favourite dishes; he washed it down with Whitbread's bottled beer drunk from a silver tankard. Anyway, I suddenly felt tears start from my eyes – I have always cried easily, and the older I get the more easily do I cry and the more pleasure I get from crying – and I said: 'I wish I'd been more use to you here, sir.' BAS grunted and said: 'Perhaps you've been more use than you think.' Next morning Derek Wigram and I set off together to Brighton station. I bought a packet of Turkish cigarettes and a copy of Nash's magazine in which I was reading a P. G. Wodehouse serial, *The Girl On The Boat*, and away we went, giggling, as we got into the compartment, about Black Ointment.

*   *   *

How does one end a book of this sort? Perhaps it's better not to try. I revisited Mowden in 1932 when I was writing a novel some of which was autobiographical. I wanted to spy out the land. My cousin John had been sent there by his mother, partly, I think because my mother had told her that I had always been very well looked after at Mowden. I found that John, a small pale-faced child of about eight, was walking round. Janet called him off and I took him for a stroll and gave him half a crown. He tells me he hated Mowden and his life wasn't made any easier when my novel was published the next year. He begged to be sent away but at first his mother wouldn't hear of it. Then, with really masterly ingenuity, he told her: 'Mrs Snell says it's a pity you wear such awfully silly hats.' That did the trick.

BAS was immersed in carpentry and a pack of Alsatians whom he'd named after Greek Gods. I remarked they'd be useful for recapturing runaway boys; he didn't seem to think that funny at all. John swears that one of these Alsatians later set on him and rolled him over and nearly savaged him; BAS kept calling out: 'Lie still, you silly boy and stop flapping that handkerchief.'

I had a quite friendly conversation with BAS. He told me that one of his sons, the middle one, Reg, was a bit of a socialist. 'I believe in people having a good time,' grunted BAS, 'but how's it going to be paid for?'

The Ape was enormously affable. I had lunch with him and Mrs Snell and nearly choked in the middle of it because I suddenly remembered how, during my last summer term, I'd had an erotic dream about her. She said rather tartly that I'd not been short of brains but was always very lazy and dreamy. After lunch it rained, so I played a game of squash with Dick Littlehales's sister who was doing a temporary matron's job, and swam in the new swimming bath. They couldn't have been nicer.